FINANCIAL

INDEPENDENCE

----- The Ultimate Guide to Exploding Your Income, Dropping out
of the Rat Race, and Achieving Financial Freedom -----

CHRIS MORGAN

I dedicate this book to everyone that has the courage to believe that financial independence is possible …
and everyone that masters the self-discipline necessary to execute it.

TABLE OF CONTENTS

About the Author

Hi,

My name is Chris and I retired at the age of 32. I am the founder of www.retiredby35.com, an early retirement and personal finance blog.

My passion in life is to educate people about saving, budgeting and investing so that they can make smarter financial decisions and work towards early retirement and financial freedom.

If you want access to a growing and value-adding content library about early retirement, personal finance topics, and investments, I highly encourage you to check out my website **www.retiredby35.com** where you can also check out my other books and sign up for my newsletter (don't worry, I'll only send high-quality content, I never sell personal information, and I don't spam!).

If you have the time and found this book useful, please be so kind and leave me an honest review in order to educate more people about early retirement and fight financial illiteracy.

Warm regards,

Chris

INTRODUCTION

FINANCIAL INDEPENDENCE

"The secret to happiness is freedom... And the secret to freedom is courage."

- Thucydides

Financial independence and early retirement are highly attractive goals for people from all walks of life, for obvious reasons. Who wouldn't like to be financially worry-free, travel wherever they want to travel, ditch horrible bosses and co-workers, and live life on their own terms?

When you are financially independent, your entire life changes. You can do what you want. You don't have to ask anyone for approval or permission for anything. You can go wherever you want, whenever you want. You have access to a lot more opportunities. You can go travel and choose another country to live in. In short, becoming financially independent liberates and empowers you beyond the wildest dreams of your imagination. It literally changes *everything*.

What Is Financial Independence?

Unfortunately, financial independence is often misinterpreted.

Financial independence - and I am going to use this term interchangeably throughout this book with other terms such as *financial freedom* or *early retirement* -, in practice, is not about spending money or living a hedonistic lifestyle at all. Quite to the contrary. Oftentimes, in my experience, people seem to think that financial independence means blowing money, flying around the world, staying in 5-star hotels and driving luxury cars. That is **not** what financial independence is all about.

In my opinion, it is exactly this *spending-focused* mindset that is the reason why not more people are financially secure and are unable to escape the rat race altogether: too many people think that financial independence means living high off the hog. Seduced by this superficial idea of financial independence, too many people don't save money, have no financial plan and no financial goals, drown in debt, have no control over their spending, and don't invest any money. For most people, money leaves their wallets quicker than it got in there. And that is exactly why not more people are financially independent!

Financial independence, at its core, is all about *freedom*. It explicitly is not about the money and what you can buy with it, and it is very important to understand this in order for you to get the most out of this book. It is about the freedom your money gives you and the opportunity it provides you with to live your life on your own terms.

Here's a good way to define financial independence:

"Financial independence is achieved when you make enough money from your investments passively so that you can comfortably cover your recurring lifestyle expenses."

It is worth mentioning that the nicest and most rewarding things in life are (and have always been) free and have nothing to do with money whatsoever: having satisfying, personal relationships, appreciating and enjoying the beauty of the world, being in good health, and helping other people ... all of these things are free and accessible to anyone that opens their eyes and hearts to the world.

Unfortunately, too many people get this fundamentally wrong and equate money with happiness when, in reality, the complete opposite is true!

The good news, however, is that financial independence can be achieved by anybody, and I mean *anybody*. It doesn't matter what job you have or what your current position in life is. If you understand and adopt the habits and strategies described in this book, there is a very good chance that you will do significantly better financially in the future than you are doing now. I also want to specifically include people here that work in standard 9-to-5 gigs and take home an average salary of between $40,000 and $60,000 annually. I was one of those people not too long ago, and if I can achieve financial independence, then so can you.

How long does it take to become financially independent?

I'd say if you start early and make financial independence the dominant goal in your life, it will take between 10 and 20 years, but you could do it a lot sooner, too. It largely depends on your earnings power, and your ability and willingness to delay consumption.

I managed to get to where I am today – living off of my investment income – in about 15 years. That being said, if I hadn't made so many dumb investment mistakes, it would have been entirely possible to have gotten there in 10 years.

My Path to Early Retirement

I studied business administration at a European university, and my major was accounting and tax accounting. I am not sure why I chose those subjects at the time. With the benefit of hindsight, I'd say that at a very young age, I had bought into the myth that money buys happiness. Therefore, what made more sense than studying business administration, the 'science of money', right?

Studying did not come easy to me, I had to work my butt off, and I mean it. The introductory math and statistics exams regularly had fail rates north of 70%, and I felt a lot of pressure to pass those exams in order to advance to my degree. As a result, I had to study a perverse amount of time, even more so later when I had to choose my major in accounting. While I pretended to enjoy my studies, I was really deeply miserable ... I was studying something I was not passionate about, essentially just because I convinced myself that that's what I had to do.

At the age of 24, three years into my studies, I flew to Thailand and Cambodia during semester break in order to explore those countries backpacker-style. I enjoyed my time traveling and experiencing not only a new culture, but a new way of life. You see, the Buddhist culture prevailing in those countries values everything we don't in the Western world: family, respect, harmony, peace of mind, happiness, etc. As I appreciated the new influences I had been exposed to, I began to seriously question the path I had chosen in my life. Why exactly was I studying what I was studying?

It was at that time that I had a life changing encounter. I rode a bicycle towards Angkor Wat, the 12th century giant temple complex of the Khmer Empire in Cambodia. As I was cycling along the road, I spotted a young girl, maybe around 20 years old, digging a water canal in the jungle. This girl did hard, physical labor in the middle of the jungle at 50 degrees Celcius. When I passed her, she stopped working, looked at me, smiled, and shouted, "Hey, how is your day today?" This girl had probably just made enough money with her work to pay for some food and water; Cambodia is one of the poorest countries in the world, yet her heart was filled with happiness. As I was cycling ahead, I could not forget this encounter. I didn't know it at the time, but this girl changed my life. I asked myself, *How is it possible that someone who is doing such hard work in such dire circumstances, in one of the poorest countries in the world, has a heart filled with happiness, but I, a comparably wealthy university student is deeply irritated about life, if not depressed? How is this possible, that people who have nothing (materially*

*speaking) are actually more happy, more fulfilled and more content with
life the way it is, than we in the West, who supposedly have everything?*

As innocent as this encounter seemed at the time, this was the point at
which my priorities in life slowly began to change: I began to value
time and happiness a lot more than status and the never-ending chase
of money. This girl, which by the way, I have never spoken to, changed
my life dramatically, and for the better. I owe her a lot for her heartfelt
smile and for setting me straight, and I wish I could go back and thank
her for what she did.

Eventually, my travels ended, and I returned to my home country to
finish my studies. I ultimately graduated with a master's degree in
accounting and started to work for a big consulting company. The job
was a nightmare: 50, 60, sometimes 70 hours a week, intense
workloads, permanent availability, a lot of pressure and stress,
weekend work, no *thank you*, and rarely any kind of genuine
appreciation. I felt I had hit a wall and wasted my life. My
dissatisfaction with my life was growing from day to day since the work
I was doing felt stupid, boring, and deeply unfulfilling.

My lack of enthusiasm for the job eventually led to the company
suggesting that I didn't make the right career decision. And, you know
what? They were right. I soon parted ways from the company, and I
had never felt more free in my life than the day I walked out of the
office leaving this mindless, soul-sucking job behind me. It felt great.

During my three years in that job, however, I socked away as much money as I possibly could; 50% of my salary went straight into my investment account every month. My bonus? I saved and invested 100% of it. Additional allowances? Same, I saved and invested everything. I invested the largest chunk of my money from February 2007 to June 2010, which, with the benefit of hindsight, was the best time to invest in stocks in at least a decade. I invested most of my money into financial and dividend-paying stocks and soon earned $1,000 or more each month in passive income. I worked two more years in Australia for a wedding company and saved another $60,000 during this time, living well below my means. When I left Australia in 2013, I had saved up more than $250,000. The growing dividend income my stock portfolio produced was more than enough for me to say goodbye to the rat race and retire in a low-cost country like Thailand.

Unfortunately, people don't see the years of hard work, sacrifice and aggressive saving that it took me to retire early. Most people simply are not willing to save this aggressively, or save at all.

Did you know that only between 1 and 5 people out of 100 are financially secure when they retire? Of course, this also means that the overwhelming majority of people are not financially secure when they enter into retirement. Why is that?

The reason is that most people (and most likely you, too!) have been conditioned by society to believe that rather than saving, it is more important to spend your money recklessly on stupid things in order to gain other people's approval. The average American adult wastes 3 to 4 hours every day (!) on social media — time that could be used much more productively when channeled into the right direction ... such as learning about investing or building an online business.

The single biggest obstacle to financial freedom, therefore, is *you*.

Way too many people out there, including you, base their entire lives on the opinions of others, which can have an incredibly stifling effect on your life and your ability to achieve financial freedom. Why do you care so much if your family, your friends, your neighbors, and your colleagues (some of whom you may only know on a first name basis), approve of you and what you do with your life?

The answer: You are insecure and seeking approval. And that is exactly what is holding you back!

The truth is that the journey towards financial independence is no picnic. It is hard work and requires an extraordinary amount of self-discipline, focus, and backbone. If you want to be financially independent, you have to learn to think for yourself. You have to stop trying to get other people to like you. You need to stop seeking approval. You should have the courage to set and follow your own goals. You need to resist peer and family pressure to spend money recklessly. You should stop trying to be cool wasting hundreds of dollars each weekend on nightclubs, bars and expensive restaurants.

Having the courage to question popular opinion (frugality vs. hedonism), controlling your impulses, and setting your own financial goals are not only crucial life skills but are absolute key to achieving financial independence. And I promise you, all it takes for you to reach your goal of financial freedom is a real commitment to follow your dream, consistent execution on your savings goals, and patience.

If you want - and I mean *really want* - to achieve financial independence, there is nothing that can stop you. At the end of the day, it all comes down to your priorities. Is it more important to you to impress other people with your possessions (your car, your house, and other status symbols), or do you actually want to make smart financial decisions that are in the best long-term interests of you and your family?

Gaining clarity over such fundamental questions is extremely important if you want to make financial independence the dominant goal in your life. If you don't really desire financial freedom and are not prepared to do the hard work (i.e. you just want stuff), then you will not achieve this goal. Like with any other goals in life - whether it is losing weight, working out more, or studying harder -, you will have to do what most people aren't willing to do. Financial independence requires a real commitment from you. If everyone could do it, it wouldn't be an accomplishment!

I can guarantee you that you will pay a price for financial independence. I am telling you this openly and straightforwardly because too many people believe there are shortcuts and "secrets" to achieving financial freedom. This is not the case. You *will* pay a personal price for it. This price will likely include discomfort and pain over the short haul as you learn new savings, budgeting and investing skills. You will probably also have to work harder and longer hours, starting a side hustle for extra income and delaying consumption. Your friends, peers, colleagues and family members may voice their disapproval and ridicule you for cutting back on entertainment expenses in order to save more money. This push-back from your social circle should be expected, though, as most insecure people tend to try to dissuade you from ambitious financial goals that fly in the face of conventional wisdom. But rest assured that you can retire early in your 30s or 40s if you make this a priority in your life ... I know heaps of people who did just that, and all of them have fairly average educational and professional backgrounds.

I want to make it very clear here that I did **not** retire early because I am so smart or educated, or because I started a super-successful business venture, gambled on some weird crypto-currency, or because I was connected to the right people. I didn't win the lottery, either.

I retired early because I did what 90% of people out there don't want to do: I saved money aggressively throughout my life, but especially in the last ten years before I dropped out of the rat race. I socked away at least 50% of my income each year for 10 years, and I want to emphasize the words "at least". Sometimes I saved 60% or more of my disposable income and I lived well below my means. As you can imagine, I was showered with ridicule from my social circle for being frugal and careful with money. It never bothered me, really, because I knew I was on the right path.

I not only saved like crazy, but I never really liked to spend much money either. Keeping the money in my bank account felt so much better than spending it on some nonsense that would only give me temporary pleasure. I never owned a car. I avoided consumer debt like the plague. I never had a credit card. I made a habit out of paying for everything in cash. I pushed back hard against impulse purchases. I budgeted my expenses meticulously and used discounts at any opportunity. I bought my first stock when I was 15 years old. I invested and reinvested into dividend-paying stocks consistently, and bought more when their prices dropped. In short, I learned to *respect* money deeply and tried to find ways to produce enough passive income to cover my lifestyle expenses instead of having to go to the terrible corporate gigs I had as a financial consultant.

In other words, I did the complete opposite of what society told me. As a result, I was never cool or popular, but also never cared about being perceived as such. With the benefit of hindsight, this saved me a *lot* of money and regret!

The truth is that I hated my job after I graduated with an MBA from a European university, so I really do understand when someone feels hopeless in their current employment situation. I despised my job so much; I was late to work every morning and my stomach would turn every day when I woke up. I hated every second of it. Every day I asked myself, *why I am doing this? Why am I going to the office? What is my purpose?* My life sucked.

I used this dissatisfaction as motivation, however, to save and invest even more money so that I could eventually drop out of the abusive rat race that I was stuck in at the time. Financial independence really became the overarching goal in my life. I became obsessed with finding a way to drop out of the rat race, forever. One of the biggest obstacles that holds people back from achieving financial freedom, in my opinion, is financial illiteracy which is a huge problem in our society and needs to be addressed.

Financial Illiteracy

Thirty percent of the U.S. population lack basic math skills, and American adults rank at the bottom end in terms of numeracy skills when benchmarked against other major industrialized countries such as Japan, Sweden, Norway and Canada. Sixty-two percent of British adults do not understand inflation, and less than 40% of people use a budget regularly to track their expenses, meaning a majority don't organize their finances at all. Eighty percent of Americans live paycheck to paycheck.

Why is that?

Simple. Most people have never learned basic money management principles and simply never question their own financial behavior! Add to the mix that way too many people, seduced by a materialistic society, live above their means and lack self-discipline to build savings consistently, and you can easily see why so many people are left behind financially. That being said, it has never been easier than today to get a grip on your financial situation, thanks to the vast proliferation of financial information on the internet. You would think that with all this knowledge at people's fingertips, you would see an improvement in overall financial literacy levels, but that does not seem to be the case. Unfortunately, most people are still effectively financially illiterate.

Financial illiteracy - which basically means that most people lack the basic skills and knowledge with respect to subjects such as budgeting, saving, investing and taxation - is a huge problem in the United States and elsewhere in the world. Not knowing how to deal with money is a problem, for obvious reasons. For one thing, not understanding basic money principles can cost you real money. Secondly, if you don't know how to keep your money, how is your financial situation ever going to improve?

Financial illiteracy, in my estimation, is one of three major reasons why only a small minority of people ever achieve financial freedom. The other reasons include being short-term oriented and spending money recklessly. If you don't want to be like the majority, those are the three areas you have to watch out for. Most people, unfortunately, lack even a superficial understanding of incredibly important financial concepts such as living below their means, avoiding consumer debt, setting budget allocations, making investments in income-producing assets consistently, and understanding the difference between the present value and future value of assets and liabilities.

Recognizing that you, too, probably lack basic financial skills is the first step towards personal growth and, ultimately, financial freedom. Admitting to yourself that you need to step up your financial game and rethink your relationship with money will be key for you to get the most out of this book.

Following the money principles in this book can dramatically and fundamentally change your life. It is in your best interest to absorb as much material as possible and return to it time and again in order to use it as a resource that accompanies your learning progress.

If you have any questions or require clarification or guidance of some sort, feel free to message me chris@retiredby35.com, or hit me up on Instagram (retiredby35) or YouTube (retiredby35).

Retirement and Savings Crisis in America

A lack of basic financial skills largely explains the dire savings and retirement crisis in America. Do you know that the average American has retirement savings of just $85,000 and that almost a quarter of citizens in the United States don't have any retirement savings at all? And do you know that financial planners typically recommend to sock away at least $1,000,000 in order to live a relatively comfortable retirement?

There is a huge problem with people's retirement preparedness. What explains widely inadequate retirement savings, whether we are talking about *early* retirement in your 30s or 40s, or *regular* retirement after your working life, is that a lot of people simply don't know how to deal with money and how to prepare for retirement. They have not yet learned essential money skills that will allow them to take charge of their financial destiny and take their lives into their own hands.

What makes matters even more difficult is that spending money gives people a quick dopamine high from a new purchase, whereas saving money consistently doesn't have this exciting effect. Furthermore, our consumer culture puts immense pressure on us to keep up with the Joneses even though the Joneses are not a very good example for people that value financial freedom over material possessions. All of these factors, financial illiteracy, poor impulse control and glorification of consumption, all are equally responsible for the poor savings situation of the average American. The good news is that we can change this.

I pride myself on authenticity which makes it imperative to stress that I am not going to sell you a magic formula or a secret of how to get rich quickly. Frankly, I detest these get-rich-quick schemes because they are utterly repulsive and disingenuous as they seek to exploit desperate people that don't have a lot of options in their lives.

Financial freedom really takes a lot of work, commitment, and planning. You will have to put in the hard work if you want to retire early, and this book right here lays out proven strategies that I have used myself in order to retire in my early thirties. Hence, this book has the ambition to give you the guidance, the knowledge and the confidence to accomplish the same thing (or other financial goals you might have and that are certainly just as valid). The core motivation for this book is to help you make smarter financial decisions that will allow you to live your life on your own terms.

With that being said, let's jump right into the content.

CHAPTER 1

LAYING THE GROUNDWORK

"If you don't know where you are going, any road will get you there."

~ Lewis Caroll

Mindset and preparation are everything. Whether you want to become an outstanding athlete, a great business person, a scientist, or, yes, someone that achieves financial freedom, it is imperative that you have the right mindset. Without the right mindset, without direction, you are floating around aimlessly in life like a vessel on the ocean without a captain.

Developing the right mindset is incredibly important because it firmly grounds you in reality and keeps your eyes focused on the prize: *financial freedom.*

Like a star athlete aiming for greatness in a competitive game, you must develop the right mindset and choose priorities that align with your long-term goals. If an athlete isn't committed to waking up early and exercising diligently, does he ever have a chance of winning a highly competitive game?

By the same token, if you aren't committed to your savings, budgeting and investing goals, do you really have a good chance of achieving financial independence?

The answer is *no*, of course.

Chances are that you are going to give up on your goals altogether, and financial freedom will forever just be a dream. A lack of commitment is a significant hurdle a lot of people will have to overcome when it comes to achieving financial independence.

Like New Year's resolutions - which typically don't last very long - too many people aren't really as committed to their resolutions or goals as they need to be. The problem with New Year's resolutions is that they are often made impulsively without a longer period of reflection. In terms of goals, most people simply don't have any. Establishing goals, however, is crucially important in order to give you direction and bring you closer to your dream, one step at the time.

In order for goals to work they need to be *specific* and *measurable*. Instead of saying something too generic like you want to "retire early and leave the rat race" , you must set specific and measurable goals such as this one: "I want to retire at 35 with $400,000 in my portfolio", or "I want to retire at 40 with my real estate portfolio valued at $1,000,000." Setting specific financial goals is important because only when they are specific can you measure your progress towards them. Ideally, you also write down your specific early retirement goals; writing your financial goals down on a piece of paper makes it 42%

more likely, according to research, that you will achieve them. Establishing specific financial goals introduces accountability, which is another added benefit that will help you bring your dream of financial freedom into reality. Without a financial road map, you won't be able to achieve financial independence.

When you first start out on your journey towards financial independence you might feel overwhelmed. Maybe you are in debt. Maybe you made the wrong career decision (like I did!). Maybe you feel crushed and hopeless. Those are entirely normal feelings in light of a massive challenge, and I went through this emotional roller coaster myself many times. Feeling overwhelmed or intimidated by ambitious financial goals such as early retirement is perfectly normal and everyone goes through this. The key to overcoming those emotions and insecurities is to just take a breath and take it slowly. Take one step at a time, and don't over-complicate things. Taking one step at the time will make things a lot easier as you travel along the road towards financial freedom.

Having the right mindset will also give you the courage to face your financial situation head-on and prepare you for the task at hand. Like with everything else in life, your mindset and attitude will determine whether or not you will achieve your financial goals.

If you need any more motivation than that, here's what having the right mindset and attitude about money will help you do:

- Build serious savings;

- Set and meet long-term financial goals;

- Tackle your debt situation (if relevant);

- Minimize wasteful spending;

- Regain control over your finances through meticulous budgeting;

- Maximize your income;

- Raise your financial IQ;

- Make better financial decisions;

- Become an investor in income-producing assets such as stocks, bonds or real estate;

- Live life independently and financially free.

Shifting Your Mindset

If you are really serious about achieving financial independence, you will have to make major life changes and need to learn to view money in a different light. You will have to go through a major attitude adjustment as well.

The right mindset and attitude towards money from now on is this: money is something that you want to *keep* and not *spend*. I need you to start to think about money not in terms of what you can *buy* with it, but in terms of what you can *earn* with it.

Once you keep your money, your money can start to work for *you*, not the other way around.

Unfortunately, a lot of people simply don't have the spending discipline and/or financial know-how that allows them to transition from a consumer mindset to an investor mindset, which is something we are going to work hard on throughout this book.

Wealthy people, who tend to be more financially-savvy than the average person, have a massive advantage here, simply because they think about money the "right" way. As a matter of fact, I have written an entire book (*9 Money Secrets of the Rich - How the Money Elite Outsmarts the Rest of Us*) about what you can learn about money from rich people. Some minor parts of this book have also been published on my blog **www.retiredby35.com** which is my preferred platform to share practical, easy-to-understand advice about how to save money, budget, invest, and grow your income with the ultimate goal being early retirement.

As you will see in the next chapter, I need you to be focused on saving money and minimizing your expenses just as much as I need you to focus on finding ways to maximize your income. And if you combine those two money strategies with a tight savings and investing game, you will be unstoppable! But first, I need you to take a hard look in the mirror.

Facing the Demon: Where Do You Stand Financially?

I shared a couple of statistics with you in the previous chapter that highlighted how utterly unprepared most Americans are when it comes to retirement. In order to understand and improve your own financial situation, it is paramount that you make an honest assessment right now about where you stand financially. While you may be hesitant to face your current financial situation, I will guarantee that in a couple of years from now, you will thank me for forcing you into action today.

Take a blank piece of paper and write down all your assets on the left-hand side of the paper and write down all your liabilities on the right-hand side of the paper. Whatever it is that you own, write it down. The list on the left-hand side will most likely include your car, the equity in your house or other properties you may own, loans you gave to somebody else, your investment portfolio and 401(k), positive bank balances, and the cash in your pockets.

Then, write down all your liabilities on the right-hand side of the paper. This list of liabilities typically includes student loan debt, auto loans, mortgages, credit card debt, personal debt, negative credit card balances, and so forth. You get the picture.

Ideally, the sum of your assets should be larger than the sum of your liabilities because that means you have a positive net worth (*Yeah!*).

Your net worth is the total that remains after you deduct the value of your liabilities from the value of your assets. Say, for instance, that you own $100,000 worth of assets (equity in primary residence, cash, 401(k) and an investment portfolio), but that you have $75,000 in debt that you need to repay (student loans, mortgage and credit card debt). After you deduct your total debt from the value of your assets, you are left with a net worth of $25,000 ($100,000 - $75,000). If the total is positive, you have a positive net worth, if the total is negative, you have a negative net worth.

If you completed the simple exercise above, you now have a complete list of your assets and liabilities in front of you. If you have a negative net worth figure, don't despair. Facing your current financial situation, no matter how bad it is, is the first step to regaining control over your finances. I will discuss more specific debt repayment strategies in Chapter 4.

I am encouraging you to do this little exercise simply so that you face your current financial reality without any excuses or rose-colored glasses. Take an honest look at your current financial situation. Running from it, avoiding it or denying it is not the solution, and it will make things worse (and more expensive) for you and your family in the future. The point here is to force you to accept reality, and that reality about your financial situation is best telegraphed through a cold, hard number that doesn't lie. Most people with debt, unfortunately, don't even know exactly how much they owe, which is a huge problem. If you don't know *how much* you owe, how could you ever hope to dig yourself out of this rabbit hole?

It takes courage to face your financial situation head-on, especially if it is messy. If you own a large amount of debt, or if you feel hopeless looking at your net worth figure that stares back at you from the paper, don't worry. If you adopt the right money mindset (that keeping money is more important than spending money), then you won't be in this financial situation forever. Taking one step at a time and playing the long game is all that you need to do here!

Make no mistake, the journey towards financial independence starts *right here*. Without fully understanding where you stand financially and reflecting on why you are in your current financial situation, there is no hope of ever getting out of debt, making smarter financial decisions, budgeting better, and starting to invest money into income-producing assets. As you progress through this book, I will walk you step-by-step through methods and "smart money strategies" that will improve your personal finance skills considerably.

So, let's start off with my favorite step towards financial freedom in the next chapter: saving money and finding ways to minimize your expenses.

Key Takeaways

- Most Americans are utterly unprepared for (early) retirement because they simply don't have the money skills. Raising your financial IQ is a core motivation for why I have written this book;

- Most people overspend, save too little (if anything at all), don't budget, have too much debt, don't invest, have poor impulse control, and don't have a long-term financial game plan. If you change all that, you will be on your way to financial independence;

- Financial freedom starts with taking an honest look at yourself, shifting your mindset, adopting smarter habits, learning about basic personal finance, and setting clear financial goals. You can start this journey today by facing the demon and calculating your net worth figure;

- Financial independence demands that you exercise self-discipline, rethink your attitude towards money, and reset your priorities. I maintain that everybody can become financially independent as long as they stick to the principles laid out in this book.

CHRIS MORGAN

CHAPTER 2

SAVING MONEY & MINIMIZING EXPENSES

"Rich people stay rich by living like they are broke and broke people stay broke by living like they are rich."

~ Dave Ramsey

Minimizing expenses plays an important and often underestimated role in building up your savings and creating long-term wealth. Living below your means is absolutely essential when it comes to creating a solid financial foundation that will allow you to retire early.

I want to be brutally honest with you here: if you don't save aggressively, it will be nearly impossible for you to retire early. I am telling you this straight up because I don't want you to have illusions about what it takes. Saving 10% of your income is a very good start and it will get you far if you stick with this habit for a long time, but most people aren't even doing that.

If you want to go freak, like I have, and retire in your 30s, you have to sock away at least half of your paycheck and adjust your lifestyle accordingly, at least over the short-term.

What exactly do I mean by "minimizing expenses"?

In a nutshell, it means that you cut back on lifestyle expenses and purposefully live frugally. You delay consumption today in order to be financially free later in your life. This is just a trade-off, like so many other things in life. It means that you prioritize saving money over spending money, which appears to be a huge challenge for a lot of people. You will have to become a saver, not a spender in order to retire early.

There are numerous reasons why you would want to cut back on spending and build savings. First of all, proving to yourself that you can build up your savings if you put y0ur mind to it is simply awesome. Second, having money in the bank can take a lot of stress out of your life. Third, opportunities for personal, professional, and financial growth often only reveal themselves to people that have the resources to take advantage of them. What use is it if you see a good investment opportunity (say, a house in your neighborhood is on the market for an attractive price, or a stock you like is on sale), but you don't have the cash to jump on the opportunity? Do you know that according to the Federal Reserve's 2018 Survey of Household Economics and Decision Making, 40% of Americans can't cover $400 in emergency expenses if disaster strikes?

And do you know why?

Because nobody ever taught us how to save money! Schools certainly don't teach it. Parents don't teach it. Universities don't teach it. Corporations want you to spend all of your disposable income on consumer goods, and hopefully go into debt. If it was up to Corporate America you would be up to your eyeballs in debt because that will ensure that you are going to show up to the rat race tomorrow!

People being unable to deal with an emergency situation, like the $400 emergency expense I just mentioned, is also the result of people making too many excuses. Few people are really willing to cut back and live below their means for an extended period of time. Too often have I heard people rationalize their inability (really: unwillingness) to save money with some of the following excuses:

- "I don't make enough money to save money!"
- "I don't have the discipline to save money!"
- "I live paycheck to paycheck."
- "Why should I restrict myself?"
- "My friends are doing it!"
- "I am young and want to enjoy my life!"
- "I want to go out with my friends and enjoy the weekend!"
- "I only live once!"
- "I deserve to treat myself well after working hard all week!"

- "The weekend is the only time I can let go, and I am going to do it!"

- "I like nice things and I want to show others what I can afford!"

- "New things make me happy!"

- "Other people like me if I do this and this."

I am sure you have heard people utter insincere and shallow excuses like these at some point in your life. Maybe you've said things like this yourself. Anyhow, in my experience, it is always broke people that insist on living *above* their means.

Now, just to be clear, there is nothing wrong with treating yourself nicely every once in a while, but only with moderation. In fact, I recommend treating yourself nicely (e.g. going out for a nice dinner) every time you reach a certain financial milestone or have made progress on a project that you have been working on. There is nothing wrong with rewarding yourself for accomplishment, and it is only fair. The point, however, is that you should be measured when it comes to "treating yourself nicely" and that you keep your savings goals firmly in mind.

With that being said, let's get to the fundamental question: what expenses do you minimize, and how do you do it?

The first step is to take a critical look at your expenditures and go through your expenses, line item by line item. A good starting point to decide whether you are wasting money on things you buy is asking yourself whether you *want* something or *need* something.

A product you *need* is a product that you really can't live without; think about toothpaste, food, or gas for your car. You really *need* those items. On the other end of the spectrum are your *wants*. They are things we *want* but do *not need*. Examples include going for an expensive meal at a fancy restaurant, buying a new smart phone even though our old one is still pretty good, or buying yet another unnecessary pair of shoes. Being able to distinguish between *wants* and *needs* is incredibly powerful when it comes to rationalizing your expenses, and it is a great way of conditioning yourself to question your purchasing decisions before you make any regretful mistakes.

I have discussed this distinction between wants and needs in some of my other books, too, and blogged about it quite a bit because it is such an important concept to internalize and apply. So, next time you feel the urge to buy something, ask yourself "Do I really *need* this, or do I just *want* this?"

Save a Ton of Money by Cutting Down on These Expenses

When you go through your monthly expenses (you will learn how to do this in Chapter 3), you will inevitably stumble over a couple of expense items that have huge savings potential. Every household, in my view, has at least 25% savings potential and that includes your household, too.

Do you disagree? Well, let's go through a couple of expenses that regularly show up in people's lives but that often don't seem to register on their radars. What follows is an (incomplete) list of expense items that may sabotage you and your family's finances:

● *Entertainment.* If you want to get out of debt and/or want to build up your savings in order to achieve your financial goals, this expense category often has the biggest savings potential. This is because when we go out, we frequently tend to spend more money than we really want to. Going out and blowing a small fortune on expensive drinks in bars and restaurants is not only not smart, but it can really set us back financially, especially if we don't keep track of our expenses;

● *Eating out.* This is another great source for saving money. If you are like most people, you like to eat out. I did the same thing when I was younger. I liked treating myself nicely, going to good restaurants and trying new food – until I started to track my expenses. Only then did I realize what insane amount of money I actually spent on eating out in restaurants, purely out of convenience and because I didn't plan any of my meals. There is a lot of savings potential here if you cut back on expensive restaurant visits, plan your meals, make sandwiches to eat at work, and make a habit out of eating a healthy, low-cost breakfast at home before you go to work;

● *Vices.* Yes, it is not easy to give up on vices, but it makes a whole lot of sense when it comes to your health and your finances. Do you smoke, drink alcohol, use recreational drugs, or gamble on a regular basis? Cutting back on those unnecessary expenses is low-hanging fruit and is something you should definitely do. If you smoke half a pack of cigarettes a day, you are on track to spend $1,043/year on your vice and $10,430 in 10 years. Is it really worth blowing this much money on essentially nothing?

● *Taking advantage of discounts/coupons.* The single best way to save money is to look for deals that allow you to avoid having to pay full retail. You see shampoo for 50% off? Take advantage of the discount and buy lots of shampoo. Do you get discounts for being a student or senior? Claim those discounts at any opportunity. If you don't know if discounts apply, don't hesitate to ask. More businesses than you would think are open to offering discounts in order to capture another customer. All you need to do is ask. Some retailers discount some of their products at the same time of each month. It is worth marking those sales days in your calendar in order to take full advantage of discount opportunities that save you real money easily;

● *Unnecessary and expensive subscriptions.* Do you have cable, Netflix and other subscriptions that cost you money on a recurring basis? Subscriptions, especially on a monthly basis, are a clever marketing trick because they cost you money regularly even when you have already stopped to use the service. Maybe there is an opportunity for you to cancel some (or all?) of your subscriptions and save you money? Remember: the easiest dollar saved is the dollar you didn't spend;

● *Gym memberships.* Do you know that about 50% of people that join a gym give up on their fitness goals within three months? Meaning there are lots and lots of people out there that pay for their gym memberships, but don't go exercise anymore, and that's a big waste of money! Either go to the gym and get your money's worth or cancel your membership. If, however, you want to get in shape but don't trust your willpower, pay on a per-visit basis, and you will avoid getting tangled up in expensive year-long membership plans that you don't use;

● *Watch out for fees.* Nowadays, everyone is looking to slap a fee on you. You know the story: cancellation fee, termination fee, overdraft fee, ATM fee, late fee, and so on. A large part of Corporate America literally just banks on you messing up because it makes their cash registers ring. An easy way to minimize expenses is to be aware of what you are *actually paying.* If you have a credit card (which I hope you do not!), make sure you understand the fees associated with the use of such card. Do you have to pay special ATM fees, late fees, etc.? Go through your bank/credit card statements line by line and see if there are any debits that you don't understand. Investigate. The more you understand, the less money you waste on unnecessary fees. If you have to pay bills at a certain date, put a reminder 1, 2, and 3 days in advance in the calendar in your phone. Stay on top of things and then people/corporations can't take advantage of you messing up!

● *Car loans.* Have you thought about financing or leasing your car? Yeah? Well, big mistake! I understand most people need transportation to get to and from work. Fair enough. The question is: do you need an expensive and fancy car for that? Probably not. Cars generally are expensive in terms of maintenance, and I highly recommend you to seek alternative means of transportation, if possible. Do not take out a

FINANCIAL INDEPENDENCE

car loan if you can avoid it. The average car payment in the United States is about $523/month which can eat into your budget quite aggressively. Do you know how much $523 invested monthly will be worth in 5 years, if invested, say, at 7%? Well, take a guess ... the answer will shock you because it is $37,460. And, just for fun, if you keep paying the $523/month for new cars throughout your life, you are missing out on $90,000 in 10 years, $267,043 in 20 years, and $615,314 in 30 years. Is your car really worth this much?

● *Transportation.* I cannot tell you how much money I saved just by relying on means of public transportation when I grew up. All my friends owned their own cars and constantly were broke because they had to pay not only for gas, but taxes, maintenance, repairs, new tires, and insurance premiums which constantly ate away at their paychecks. If you have access to public transportation or if you can share a ride with someone, you will save a LOT of money over time that you can use to repay debt or invest into income-producing assets such as stocks or real estate. And, really, who cares if you drive an old shitty car that does the job? Focus on the growth of your savings account instead of obsessing and worrying about what people will say about your ride. Downgrade your car if necessary. Nobody cares about it much as you, anyways!

● *Impulse buys.* Do you have a proclivity to buy stuff you don't really need impulsively? Maybe now is the time to face your weaknesses and commit yourself to spending money more carefully going forward. Refuse to make impulse purchases at supermarkets, department stores, or e-Commerce stores, and only buy products after you have carefully examined whether you really *need* the item (*wanting* it is not enough!);

● *Use price comparison apps.* Make a habit out of price-checking at any opportunity, especially if you know you are weak when it comes to making impulse buys. Price-checking items you intend to purchase is a great way of lowering unnecessary expenses. You can just pull out your smart phone and go to Amazon.com or Walmart.com and check how much the item you desire costs there. Due to the large scale of these companies, they often tend to offer the best retail prices, so if you really do need a product, make sure you take the time to research the best price;

● *Expensive hobbies.* Expensive hobbies are another area that is worth scrutinizing for wasteful spending. Lots and lots of savings potential here;

● *Gadgets.* Are you one of those people that feels compelled to regularly update their smart phones, tablets, iMacs, gaming computers, and smart TVs? People with a weakness for new technology products spend a considerable amount of their money on new gadgets and computers that quickly become obsolete as new technologies and faster processors emerge in the market. Constantly upgrading your tech suite is not a smart move and becomes very expensive and wasteful over extended periods of time. Don't play this game! What's more important to you? Having the newest iPhone or actually working towards your ambitious financial goals to retire early and be financially free?

● *Credit cards.* I hate credit cards, and I have never had one. They are a trap and super toxic because they seduce people into overspending. Credit cards entice you to make impulse buys and buy things you can't really afford; if you could afford them, you wouldn't have to use a credit card! Plus, credit card issuers and banks charge you ridiculous fees for using them. Is it really worth paying 15% interest and late fees because you felt the need to buy a 2-inch larger smart TV with a credit card? Credit cards entrap people, and too often the use of them marks the beginning of a devastating debt spiral. Pay in cash whenever you can. Paying in cash really forces you to question whether a purchase makes sense or not. When you feel the pain associated with seeing your hard-earned cash leave your wallet, only then you will be much more careful and considerate with your money;

● *Your wardrobe.* People spend a ridiculous amount of money on clothes and accessories these days. Sure, you want to look nice and dress a certain way. Nothing wrong with that. But if you spend more than 5% of your monthly disposable income on buying new clothes, bags, and accessories, maybe it is time to gain some perspective and clarity over your priorities. You can either spend a fortune on your wardrobe and appearance or invest the money into a portfolio of income-producing assets that will pay you while you sleep. Again, it's all about priorities here; you decide!

● *Gifts.* I have friends of mine that spend hundreds of dollars each year on presents for other people, friends, colleagues, bosses, girlfriends, you have it. Many of those arrangements are reciprocal. You know the drill: we buy each other Christmas or birthday presents and then we all pretend that we like them! The truth of the matter is that most presents we receive are garbage and a total waste of money, and the same is probably true for presents we give to others. Hence, I dramatically cut back on making promises to exchange gifts on various holidays, most of which are pure inventions anyways. I save and invest my money, my would-be gift receivers don't waste their time and money either, and my house is less cluttered as a result. Everybody wins!

● *Extravagant vacations.* Again, this is an easy one, and there is a lot of potential to save a considerable amount of money here. If you feel the need to go on one lavish vacation and blow through 6 months worth of savings, you may want to be honest and ask yourself what your real priorities are. I know lots of people that didn't go on a vacation for 5 or 10 years simply because they hustled, built their businesses and invested every dime they could get their hands on. This is a rather extreme approach to life, obviously, but one that's the complete opposite of what most people would do. Keep in mind, though, that this kind of focused hustle and effort will reward you later in life when you are early retired and sipping a cocktail on a beach in Bali while all your friends and coworkers are still showing up to those jobs…;

● *Your wedding.* That's right! I know, this one is not going to make me popular, but we need to talk about it in all seriousness. I am not here to pretend that I am your new best friend, but someone needs to tell you the truth, even when it hurts. I worked for a wedding company in Australia for 2 years and I have regularly seen people ~~waste~~ spend the equivalent of $25,000 or $30,000 for essentially a one-day party and an exhaustive photo-op. Your wedding day may be a special day in your life and worth remembering, but is this memory worth $30,000? Do you really want to spend $30,000 or more on a party? Why not scale it down a bit and make a down payment for a house instead, or pay back student loans?

● *Travelling.* If you plan on going on a road trip, you can save a LOT of money just by planning ahead and booking flights and hotels as early as circumstances allow. Often, airlines give away tickets for 50% off or more when you book well in advance (more than 2 or 3 months), and sometimes you can save even more money than that. If you have travel plans, it really pays to make an itinerary ahead of time and lock in discounted airline ticket prices. The same is true for hotel rooms. I have had great success calling up hotels and straight-up asking them for a discount, offering to pay in advance straight to the hotel as opposed to using one of the travel platforms that carry their listings (and take commissions). I have been able to save 15-20% on my expected hotel bills just by planning ahead and asking hotels for a discount. Just ring them up, ask to talk to management or the reservation department. The worst thing they can say is "No," and even then you haven't lost anything. If you don't ask, you won't get a discount! Of course, you must be sure that you are really going to travel at the dates you book as hotels offering discounts are unlikely to refund you the money in case your travel plans fall by the wayside;

● *Expensive (and useless) advisers.* The average person/investor doesn't need a lot of advisers. Nonetheless, people pay way too much money in fees for their financial consultants, financial planners, banks, and mutual funds. As we will see in Chapter 6 and 7, I recommend people to empower themselves by managing their own investment portfolios, or take the auto-pilot way by investing in exchange-traded funds. It is not as hard as it looks.

These are just a couple of examples in order to show you specific expense categories that have potential to cut your expenses and save you a lot of money. The truth is that you can find ways to save money in ALL areas of your life... if you only care enough to look. The question really is: how serious are you about your savings goals and financial independence?

At the end of the day, life is simply a trade-off. How aggressively you push for saving money and cutting expenses is up to you, of course. Remember, though, that you will be compensated richly in the future for the sacrifice and commitment you are showing today. It really is up to you what your priorities are, but I would encourage you to put the emphasis on living below your means and minimizing your expenses for the benefit of a financially worry-free future.

Should You Spend $5 Daily on Your Cafe Latte or Not?

There is a passionate discussion about this topic going on in the personal finance community and among bloggers. The central question is: "Should you spend $5 on your cafe latte, or should you save that money and put it towards your savings?"

The answer to this question is crystal clear, at least to me: save the money!

But just to be sure, let's do some math to back up my claim!

Assume you drink a cafe latte 5 times a week that sets you back $5 each time. That's $25 a week, $100 a month, $1,200 a year, $6,000 in 5 years and $12,000 in 10 years.

$12,000 in a decade wasted on drinks! And that's if you don't invest the money! Hopefully, though, as you progress reading through this book, you will be all fired up about saving and investing money and start to think about what is commonly referred to as the *future value of money.*

So, let's say I got you to trust me right now and you turn your coffee addiction into a savings plan. What is the future value of your savings plan?

Here are the stats.

If you consistently make $100/month contributions to an investment account or low-cost exchange-traded fund for 10 years, assuming a 7% investment return and assuming no taxes (for the sake of simplicity), the $12,000 you made in deposits will grow to approximately $17,208 in 10 years.

The final amount of $17,208 is referred to as the *future value* of your investment. This is the amount of money you would have in your investment account after 10 years if you made regular $100/month contributions throughout this time. So, as you can see, a seemingly small expense that so many people carelessly dismiss as negligible has actually all of a sudden become very significant in financial terms!

It is important that you truly understand the point I am making here: just by saving the money you would have spent on an item as seemingly irrelevant as a cafe latte and investing the money consistently, after 10 years you will have saved up enough money for you to make a down payment on a house or an income-producing investment property! Let that sink in for a minute. How does your cafe latte taste now?

I like a coffee just as much as the next person, but is this habit really worth $17,000 over a 10-year period? $17,000 is a really hefty sum of money to spend on coffees, wouldn't you agree?

Small amounts of money do add up fast and not understanding this is probably the single biggest mistake people make, in my opinion, when it comes to saving money and building wealth systematically.

And, just for the sake of argument here, imagine what you could really do for yourself financially if you are fully committed to your dream of achieving financial freedom and putting all of your expenses under a microscope. Imagine what you could do for yourself and how quickly you could retire if you saved not just $100/month by cutting out your coffee habit, but by putting $500, $1,000 or $2,500 each month into assets that produce a recurring stream of income for you. If you prioritize savings, you will be on the fast track to financial independence.

Always remember:

"Most people *underestimate* the power of saving small amounts of money consistently and *overestimate* their ability to save money later in life."

You see, people that encourage you to keep spending $5/day on your coffee habit, or dismiss saving small amounts of money as silly or meaningless, tend to focus more on the "earnings" side of financial independence, meaning their argument is that you should concentrate on maximizing your income instead of pinching pennies.

I disagree wholeheartedly with this notion for two specific reasons. For one, people grossly and negligently underestimate how powerful it is to save small amounts of money consistently over time. Small change put away consistently piles up very quickly. And two, dismissing $5/day as an insignificant expense that is not worth fussing about just shows me that absolutely crucial money lessons have not yet been learned by the people that make those suggestions. Postponing to save money is a cardinal sin and closely related to a phenomenon called "lifestyle creep".

Lifestyle creep means that your living expenses increase as your income goes up, which makes intuitively sense, right? Say, for instance, that you used to be perfectly happy driving an old Toyota Sedan to work. But now that you have gotten a promotion and a salary increase, you can't possibly be seen anymore in a Toyota. You feel compelled to broadcast your increase in earnings power to the world by purchasing a brand-new BMW.

The problem here should be obvious to you: as you upgrade your lifestyle in lockstep with your increased income, you will see an increase in expenditures and you likely won't be able to save any money, even though your financial fortunes have improved. If you have not learned to save money on a small income, you are not going to save money on a big income!

While it is true that there are two ways to attain financial freedom - lowering your expenses and maximizing your income (a subject I am going to address in more detail in Chapter 5) -, the *smartest* way to go about it is to value both sides of the equation: try to be smart with the money you have and simultaneously seek other income sources that supplement your main income.

Just focusing on one part of the equation, i.e. maximizing income, is a huge mistake, in my opinion. Proving to yourself that you can indeed save money consistently is an achievement in itself, something to be proud of, and it will boost your confidence. Being able to save money systematically is a character-building endeavor that exercises your self-discipline muscle and it will serve you for the rest of your life!

I cannot tell you into how many people I have run into in my life that treated my respectful approach towards money dismissively and laughed at me regularly for "restricting myself," or being "boring." "Why do you save 50% of your income?", or "What are you saving for if you don't enjoy your life?", were some of the criticisms that were thrown at me.

Typically, my standard response was: "So that I can drop out of the rat race and retire early," or, "So that I don't have to work in the same job as you all my life." These answers, without exception, were often met with a blank stare which, as the prudent observer will notice, reveals cognitive dissonance. You see, most people in the rat race never question why they are in it. They cannot understand people that don't just live for the weekend. These people have a deep-seated need to be surrounded by people that share their limiting mindset: get a dull 9-to-5 gig, spend money foolishly, and get drunk on the weekend.

People tend to respond with disbelief and ridicule when they encounter approaches to life that differ from their own. Too many people simply can't fathom the idea that taking a shitty job and getting into debt to buy a lot of toys is not a compelling way to live life. I know, it's a real shocker!

I always used ridicule, denial, and critical questioning as motivating forces to double down on my efforts to retire early because I knew deep in my heart that I was doing the right thing and that my efforts would eventually pay off. The last thing you should do, if you experience the same, is take criticism or ridicule to heart. I have been laughed at for being frugal and committed to saving/investing money for so long now that I am starting to wonder if something is wrong with me every time someone *doesn't* try to put me down.

What you should keep in mind here, though, is that only people with small minds, no savings, no goals, and no guidance will laugh about you when you sock away your coffee money. You will never meet a person with large goals and serious accomplishments that will try to belittle your ambitions. Remember this next time when work colleagues, friends, neighbors, and acquaintances feel the need to try to take you down a notch when their hear about your early retirement goals. Don't bother arguing and defending your point of view. It is not personal. They simply don't know any better.

Ideally, keep your financial goals to yourself and keep your eyes firmly locked on the price: the building of an investment portfolio that throws off enough passive income that you can live off of for the rest of your life. Believe me, sooner rather than later, people will show up in your life telling you how *lucky* you are to retire early. Nobody sees and acknowledges the sacrifice and the will power it takes to delay consumption, to pay down debt aggressively, to meticulously budget and track your expenses. Don't expect any recognition.

Let the results speak for themselves, and don't get distracted from your financial goals by people that don't share the same vision as you.

Saving Money, $1 at a Time

You can change your entire world and outlook on life by saving *one dollar at a time*. You don't have to have it all figured out as you begin your savings journey. In fact, you can use a couple of super-simple strategies in order to get started and skyrocket your savings over time.

1. Use Automated Savings Plans (Pay Yourself First)

Automated savings plans automatically deduct a specified percentage from your paycheck, say 5 or 10%. Since this portion of your income is now automatically deposited into a dedicated savings account, you never see the money in your regular bank account and, thus, avoid the temptation to spend it. The guiding principle here is that you spend only the money that is left after saving and do not save what is left after spending! The idea: you pay yourself first!

Pro-Tip: If you still end up spending/wasting a lot of money, crank that savings percentage up to 15%, 20%, or even more than that.

2. Save Money Consistently

Key to having success financially and meeting your long-term financial goals in order for you to retire early - I can't emphasize this enough - is to save money *consistently*.

Saving money regularly is key, and the more money you save the better. Consistency means that you put money aside every month, no matter your personal or financial situation. There should be no excuses. That's why automated savings plans are so awesome: you save money automatically and are not tempted to spend your money as you never see it in your regular bank account anyways.

3. Save Money Early

The earlier you start to save money, the more time your money has to work for you. The compounding effect (which we will discuss in Chapter 9) is absolutely incredible because it turbocharges your ability to create wealth long-term! Starting to save money early is probably the single biggest advantage you have over everybody else when it comes to building a sizable nest egg. If you are a teenager or a college student in your early 20s, saving $50 or $100 a month and investing it will be an absolute game changer ten, twenty years from now. It may not feel like it is, but believe me, it will be!

Every dollar counts. If you can't save $20 a week or a month, but just $10, that's fine. The point here is that you get started, and that you learn to build a new habit.

I always recommend people to save at least 10% of their income as soon as they get their paychecks. 10% out of a $2,000 salary is just $200 a month that will go straight into your savings account (the one that will finance your dream one day!). That's just $50 a week, and it's really not that much.

Once you start saving money one dollar at a time, you will be positively surprised by how quickly money actually accumulates in your savings account. And as you go along on your journey towards financial freedom, I bet that you will come up with more and more creative ideas of how to save even more money. More often than not, people that start off with saving just 5 or 10% of their paychecks find ways to sock away 20 or 30% or even more of their incomes because they really get into it. (Remember, I said before, every household has a least 25% savings potential.) Saving money is nothing more but a skill, and it gets easier the longer you are doing it.

Strategically Building Savings with Retirement Accounts

In the past, American workers could rely on a three-part retirement system consisting of employer-funded retirement (a corporate pension), social security, and their own investments that would provide them with income once they retired.

Standard corporate pensions are often referred to as *defined benefit plans*. Defined benefit plans were the norm in Corporate America 40 or 50 years ago, but, with few exceptions, they have all but vanished from the retirement landscape.

Defined benefit plans would typically be provided by large employers such as General Electric or Ford Motor. If you worked for one of those companies, they would make regular payments to a pension plan over the time of your employment and the pension plan would then invest the money until you retired. Once you reached your retirement age, the pension plan would pay you a monthly pension, usually for the rest of your life.

The key feature of a defined benefit plan is that the corporation carries all of the investment risk since it makes an explicit pension promise (a certain percentage of a worker's last salary would be paid as a pension in perpetuity). If the pension plan was underfunded, the employer had to make up for the shortfall by providing additional capital. In short, in a defined benefit plan the employer took all the risk and the employee got a pension that allowed for a high degree of financial security.

That was in the old world.

Corporations have been gradually moving away from providing company-funded pensions for their workers, partly due to decreasing union membership and an associated decline in union bargaining power. Instead, corporations have started to shift the burden of retirement planning and funding to their employees. What has emerged as a solution to this problem are so called *defined contribution plans*. That's your 401(k).

In a defined contribution plan, the employer's only obligation is to make financial contributions to the plan. The employer does **not** make a pension promise and the employer is not responsible for the future value of the investments in the plan. Contrary to a defined benefit plan, the investment risk in a defined contribution plan lies entirely with the employee.

In other words, if you are not lucky enough to take part in a defined benefit plan, it is entirely your responsibility now to prepare for retirement, and you are well advised to do this *as soon as possible*.

If you are currently working for a U.S. company, chances are that your employer does not offer a defined benefit plan, but only a standard 401(k) retirement plan. Though 401(k) retirement plans, from an employee perspective, are a second-best solution to their retirement planning needs, they nonetheless allow employees to build up their retirement savings strategically over time.

So, let's discuss this savings vehicle first.

Retirement Account #1: 401(k)

A 401(k) is an employer-sponsored retirement plan and is a savings/investment/retirement vehicle that allows the employee to invest in a mix of different assets with financial aid from the employer. Think of a 401(k) as a tax-advantaged holding account which invests in a range of assets (stocks, bonds, funds etc.) that you will have to select.

A typical 401(k) retirement plan is funded by pre-tax paycheck deductions, and the emphasis here is on *pre-tax*. This means that your contributions are tax-deductible, which in turn implies that you will pay less income taxes in the year you are making those contributions.

Over the life of your 401(k), the money you put into your retirement plan grows tax-deferred, which means your investment value can grow more quickly over time as Uncle Sam does not tax your gains as long as you don't touch your investments. However, once you withdraw money from your 401(k), which is typically when you retire, your withdrawals will be taxed at your income tax rate.

The important thing with 401(k) plans is that there are contribution limits set by the IRS - the Internal Revenue Service - that will tell you exactly how much money you can put into your retirement plan each year. The 2019 employee contribution limit is $19,000, which means you can deduct up to $19,000 a year from your taxable income and invest it into your 401(k). Employees that are age 50 and older get the $19,000 pre-tax deduction but in addition also get a $6,000/year "catch-up contribution", meaning that the maximum employee contribution sits at $25,000. The limit on combined employer and employee 401(k) plan contributions in 2019 is $56,000 ($62,000 including catch-up contributions).

Catch-up contributions are special rules that allow people who are age 50 and over to put more money towards their retirement plan in order to prepare adequately for retirement. Contribution limits are adjusted annually in order to account for the effects of inflation.

Most employers offer what's called *contribution matching* and they are the two most important words for you (if you are an employee) when it comes to utilizing the full power of your 401(k) as a savings vehicle.

Many employers offer to match your contributions to your retirement plan as an incentive for you to save for retirement. Say, for instance, you have decided to put 5% of your $50,000 annual salary into your 401(k) and your employer offers a 50% match up to 5% of your pre-tax salary. This means that if you contribute $2,500 ($50,000 x 0.05) to your 401(k), your employer will contribute another $1,250 ($2,500 x 0.5) to your retirement savings plan.

This is FREE money, and you should not leave it on the table!

Here are a couple of things to keep in mind when dealing with your 401(k):

- It is important that you familiarize yourself with your employer's specific 401(k) plan and the guidelines that apply. Do you know the specifics of your employer's contribution matching?;

- Though 401(k) plans are managed by specialized companies, *you* have to decide what investments you make within the plan (how much money you allocate to stocks, bonds, funds, commodities etc.);

- 401(k) plans are portable, meaning that if you leave a job, you can take your 401(k) with you;

- There are special withdrawal and "hardship rules" governing your 401(k) that apply if you lose your job, for example;

- If you withdraw funds from your 401(k) early, you are subject to tax penalties depending on your age and 401(k) plan rules;

- 401(k)s are heavily regulated in order to protect employees;

- You typically have until April the 15th to make your 401(k) contributions.

The IRS website (www.irs.gov) is the preferred resource for you if you want to know more about 401(k) retirement plans, rules governing these savings vehicles, and contribution limits, which are updated annually.

Retirement Account #2: Traditional IRA

A traditional IRA account is another individual retirement account that you can use as a savings and retirement vehicle. Contributions to the account are made with pre-tax dollars and your investments in the account can grow tax-deferred until you make withdrawals, which is typically when you retire from the workforce. Withdrawals from a Traditional IRA during retirement are taxed at your ordinary income tax rate.

However, should you decide to make a withdrawal before the age of 59½ you will have to pay a 10% early withdrawal penalty. When you reach age 70½ you *must* make minimum distributions and are no longer eligible to contribute to your traditional IRA. The contribution limit for 2019 is $6,000 if you are below the age of 50, and $7,000 if you are age 50 or above.

Retirement Account #3: Roth IRA

A Roth IRA is yet another way for you to save for your retirement. A Roth IRA differs significantly from the 401(k) employer-sponsored retirement plan and the Traditional IRA that we just discussed. The main difference is that with a Roth IRA you make contributions to a retirement account with *after-tax dollars*. As a result, you will *not* get a tax deduction on your contributions to your Roth IRA. The upside, however, is that your investment grows tax-free and that qualified withdrawals from your Roth IRA plan are also tax-free when you retire.

Qualified withdrawals are distributions that meet certain IRS standards. As with other retirement savings accounts, the IRS is setting annual contribution limits that apply to your Roth IRA. For 2019, your total annual contributions to all of your traditional and Roth IRAs cannot be more than $6,000 if you are under age 50 ($7,000 if you are over age 50), or your taxable compensation for the year, if your compensation was less than this dollar limit.

Roth IRA withdrawals are tax-free if certain conditions are met. Those conditions are:

1. You are withdrawing an amount equal to your contributions;

2. You are above the age of 59½ and you have had your Roth IRA for at least five years;

3. You met certain other requirements (disabled, first time home buyer).

What Retirement Account Is Right for You?

Well, that depends.

It depends on your age, your personal situation, your income, your current and estimated future tax rates, your family situation, your living expenses, and so on.

As a bare minimum, I highly recommend contributing regularly to your 401(k) retirement plan. 401(k) plans offer a lot of advantages including tax deductions, tax-deferred growth, and contribution matching.

Make sure that you take full advantage of contribution matching from your employer and get the maximum match that is possible under your employer's 401(k) plan. Anything else, frankly, would be really stupid. Your employer gives you free money which can be invested for decades. It's really a no-brainer!

In addition, Roth IRAs are also a great way to prepare for your retirement. Earnings on your investments within your Roth IRA grow tax-free. Making contributions to a Roth IRA makes sense for someone that expects to have a higher tax rate in the future compared to today. I always recommend to consult a tax professional to assist you in determining which kind of retirement plan makes the most financial sense to you since so many different factors play into the decision to choose an account.

Lastly, you can also simply take your after-tax pay and invest some of it into dividend-paying stocks that you keep in your personal investment portfolio, which is the way I do it. Again, your mileage may vary, so by all means, if you need more tailored advice with respect to choosing the best retirement account for you, don't hesitate to enlist the help of a qualified retirement planner and/or tax professional, or ask your employer for guidance.

How Much Should You Have Saved?

In short, the more the better.

Conventional personal finance wisdom calls for people to have saved up a multiple of their annual salary, depending on age. If you are a 35-

year old you should have saved up 2x your annual salary, if you are a 40-year old you should have socked away 3x your annual salary, if you are 50 years of age you should have at least 6x your salary in a combination of savings and dedicated retirement accounts.

Say, for instance, that you are a 35-year old making $100,000/year working for a digital marketing agency, then your total savings ideally should be about $200,000 ($100,000 x 2). If you are a 40-year old contractor working for the government making $75,000/year, you should have socked away $225,000 ($75,000 x 3) in a combination of savings, investments and retirement accounts.

If you are shooting for early retirement, obviously, you need to save faster than most people and, preferably, start much earlier than others, which is why it is so important that people below the age of 25, or even better below 20, get this book into their hands.

These rules are not carved in stone, though. When I graduated from high school, I had saved up about $50,000, give or take, through a combination of hustling in odd jobs and investing, but I lost a good chunk of it during the stock market wipe-out of 1999 and 2000. I had $250,000 saved up altogether when I dropped out of the rat race at 32, but, in fairness, I also want to mention that I did not have any dependents, I had no student loans, no car loans, and no credit card debt. I generally recommend people to consider early retirement once they hit the $500,000 wealth level as singles, or the $750,000 wealth level as couples, if they live in a low-cost country. If you live in a high-cost country such as the United States, the United Kingdom or

Australia, you need to at least double those amounts to $1,000,000 for singles and $1,500,000 for couples.

These are only rough numbers, of course, and they just serve as a general guideline because people's expenses differ wildly depending on where they live, how big their families are, what insurances they have and how much taxes they have to pay. As a general rule, however, the more money you can put aside, the sooner you are going to be able to retire early. The best time to start saving money was yesterday. The second-best time to start is TODAY.

Emergency Savings

You definitely need to set some money aside for emergencies. Emergencies can happen to anyone at any time, and having some savings to fall back on is crucial in order to protect you and your family from financial catastrophe. Emergencies can include unforeseen medical expenses due to sickness or accidents, a car that needs to be repaired immediately, or a broken washing machine that needs to be replaced. Other more serious emergencies include you losing your job (and your income) or having to deal with the death of a family member. I recommend stashing away 3-6 months' worth of living expenses in an emergency fund in order to deal with such unforeseen expenses.

Key Takeaways

● Minimizing expenses is a *complimentary* strategy to maximizing income when it comes to financial freedom and you should use the power of both approaches in order to reach your financial goals. Whatever you do, you must learn to live below your means in order to build up your savings systematically;

● You MUST prioritize saving over spending money in order to change the trajectory of your life. If you want to retire early, you must be an aggressive saver;

● Go through the list of savings examples I have outlined in this chapter. Lots of them will apply to you and point you to potentially significant savings;

● Carefully analyze your monthly expenses. List your expenses line item by line item and identify wasteful spending. Most households have at least 25% savings potential. Critically evaluate your expenses and start building the habit of saving money;

● Saving small amounts of money consistently is an absolute game changer. Small savings add up quicker than you would think, and you can really turbocharge your journey to financial freedom if you commit yourself to the challenge. Save money regularly, even if it's only $5 or $10 a day or week. You may not believe me, but trust me, it will make all the difference in the world five or ten years from now;

- Saving money regularly through automated savings plans will help you to work systematically towards your dream of financial freedom;

- If broke people laugh about you and your early retirement goals, I guarantee you that you are on the right track;

- Stick to your savings goals in the face of criticism, disbelief and ridicule from friends, colleagues and family members and watch people go from "Why are you doing it?" to "How did you do it?";

- Retirement plans such as 401(k)s are a great way to build savings as they come with multiple benefits including income tax deductions, tax-deferred growth in the investment account, and contribution matching;

- Consult a certified financial planner and/or tax professional to help you determine the ideal combination of retirement plans and retirement accounts;

- 401(k) employer-sponsored retirement plans as well as Traditional IRAs demand pre-tax contributions and qualified withdrawals are classified by the IRS as taxable income. Roth IRA contributions are made with after-tax dollars and qualified withdrawals are tax-free;

- Aim to have saved up at least twice your annual salary by 35. If you want to retire early, you need to double your efforts and sock away at least $500,000 as a single, or $750,000 as a couple (if you are living in a low-cost country). You need to at least double those amounts if you are living in a high-cost country;

● Keep 3-6 months' worth of living expenses in an emergency fund;

● Think long-term, and don't be discouraged by the size of the mountain you are about to climb. Save $1 at a time. And remember: the vast majority of people never save any money to begin with because they *underestimate* the power of saving small amounts of money consistently and *overestimate* their ability to save money later in life. Don't make this mistake!

Chapter 3

Budgeting

"A year from now you will wish you had started today."

~ Karen Lamb

Minimizing your monthly expenses is an intuitive and straightforward way for you to save money. But how do you know exactly *where* you are spending too much money? How can you identify areas in your life in which you are overspending?

This where a budget comes in!

Budgeting, in a nutshell, is the systematic tracking of your income and your expenses over time, in order for you to understand what you are spending your money on. Budgeting provides context and tells you where your money is going. At its most fundamental level, budgeting is all about raising your awareness, and it is inseparable from saving money.

Budgeting has multiple benefits and more often than not is a really eye-opening experience for people that have never done it before.

The good news is that budgeting doesn't cost you anything (other than time) and it has a lot of upside.

Specific budgeting advantages include:

- You (re)gain control over your financial situation and your life;

- You will see your future more clearly as budgeting structures and systematizes your finances;

- You can track your progress with respect to your savings and budgeting goals;

- You begin to understand what you are spending money on;

- You can identify areas of problematic spending that have held you back in the past;

- You can take corrective action yourself;

- You will become super systematic with your finances and increase your financial IQ;

- You will find creative ways to cut back on unnecessary expenses;

- Budgeting helps you transition to a saving/investment mindset;

- It will help you save money;

- It will give you confidence and hope.

Budgeting really sets you straight financially and you will learn a lot about your current financial situation. Plus, there is absolutely no downside to budgeting other than investing a little bit of time at the end of the day to track your expenses.

The cardinal rule of budgeting is that you don't spend more money than you make. Simple, right? Say your income is $2,000/month. Deduct 10% ($200/month) of this income that you automatically put into a dedicated savings account based on the explanations provided in the previous chapter. After deducting your savings, you should not be spending more than $1,800 in any given month. If you spend more money than $1,800, you are overspending, which is also often called being "cash flow negative".

Of course, sometimes it happens that you overspend because of one larger expense, say an insurance payment, a medical expense or a home/car repair. However, if you find that you overspend regularly, this is a red flag that you don't have your finances under control! As a general rule, you would want to avoid being cash flow negative (i.e. spending more money than you are bringing in) more than two months in a row. If this happens, you need to adjust your spending behavior or look for alternative income sources to improve your cash situation.

Why You Need a Budget

Every (successful) company uses a budget, and for good reason. Budgeting includes setting financial goals and making sure that you are on track to reach them. In a free market economy, corporations sell products and services in the marketplace and try to turn a profit by providing cost-effective solutions to their customers' problems.

In order to be successful in the market, companies use budgets as an essential tool to plan their actions so that they can reach their financial goals, which typically is to make a profit. Without a detailed, thought-out financial plan, a company has no chance of succeeding in the market over the long-term.

Whether you are a corporation or an individual doesn't matter. Budgeting gives structure to your finances and allows you to move closer and closer to your long-term financial goals.

Imagine a situation in which you have credit card debt and your finances are in disarray. How can you ever hope to get out of debt if you don't know exactly where you stand financially and how much money you spend regularly? How much money do you spend on groceries each month? Insurances? Accommodation? Transportation? If you don't know the answers to these questions, keep reading, I specifically wrote this chapter for you.

If you are in debt, a carefully developed budget will allow you to repay debt faster than you ever thought possible. I know people that after they started to carefully budget their expenses, were able to triple their debt payments in a very short period of time. Those people are NOT an exception. Once you actually understand where your money goes, it will be much easier for you to stop the debt spiral and regain control over your finances and your life.

Let's Do It: You Are Learning to Budget Now

In its most simple format, a budget lists your income and all of your expenses on one sheet of paper. At this point, I would recommend you to go to my blog www.retiredby35.com and download my *Budgeting Made Easy* template that will make the budgeting exercise a lot less intimidating for you. It's totally free and you can immediately use it once you save it to your computer, tablet or phone. I have used the exact same budgeting sheet for the last ten years of my life and meticulously included all expenses, no matter how small. Both beginners and semi-experienced budgeteers should be able to find value in this budgeting sheet. Go and get it :)

Here's a screenshot!

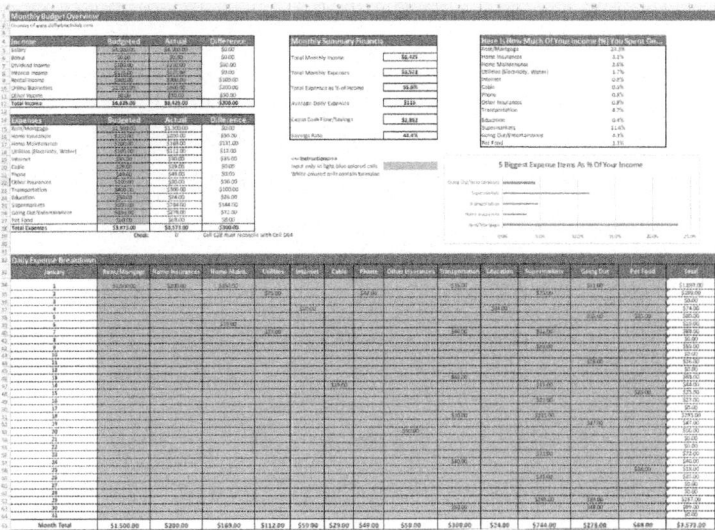

Ideally, download the template and print it out. In order to get the most out of this budgeting exercise, you need to get your hands dirty; don't just look for an easy way and let some app do all the budgeting work for you. The learning experience will be much better if you actually do the work yourself.

Fill the budgeting template out at the end of each day (at the computer or manually by hand if you have a print-out), and take a close look at the numbers and totals that reflect your actual life.

Personally, I love crunching numbers, calculating ratios and categorizing expenses (and as a trained financial analyst, I should be able to do those things!). That said, though, I recognize that not everybody likes to get into the nitty-gritty stuff of budgeting and that most people look for an easy solution to their budgeting needs … and that's why I came up with a nicely formatted *Budgeting Made Easy* template.

In the Excel sheet, you will see that I track expenses on a *daily* basis. If I go out and spend just half a dollar in a 7/11, rest assured that at the end of the day I will put those 50 cents in the right column of my Excel sheet.

The reason should be obvious to you by now: you want to understand exactly what is happening with your money and in order to do so you have to be correct. If you let things slide and are not really on top of tracking your expenses on a daily basis, you will make errors that will ultimately defeat the entire purpose of this budgeting exercise. If you have an error-ridden, poorly-maintained budgeting sheet, the decisions you derive from your cash flow statement will be equally poor as well.

As I said, I track my expenses on a daily basis, and I highly recommend you do the same. It only takes a couple of minutes at the end of each day to type my expenditures into my budgeting sheet. I suggest that you collect all the receipts you get throughout the day and type the numbers in the corresponding columns of the Excel sheet. Say, for instance, that you spent $10 on food, $25 on paying your cell phone bill and $50 to fill your car up with gas. Your job will be to fill in the corresponding numbers $10, $25, $50 into the correct columns (supermarkets, phone and fuel) in the budgeting sheet for the correct day.

The budgeting sheet is extremely powerful because it makes it incredibly easy for you to see how much money you have been spending on each expense category in any given week/month/year. The budgeting sheet calculates totals for "daily expenditures" horizontally (the amount of money you spent in a single day), and it calculates running totals for "monthly categories" vertically (the amount of money you spent in a month on, say, transportation, utilities or food). This way you can identify exactly how much money you spent per day, how much money you spent on any given category so far this month, and how much money you spent in total/on average per day.

Lastly, the Excel sheet calculates a number of ratios and depicts your expenses by category graphically which helps you understand things more quickly (and it makes things easier on the eyes).

I have prepared and formatted the *Budgeting Made Simple* template in such a way that getting started is super easy. All you need to do is put in your expense figures in the appropriate expense categories, and all sums and ratios calculate automatically. All you have to do, really, is to collect your receipts, sit down for 5 minutes at the end of the day and do simple data entry.

My Top 5 Budgeting Tips

Here are my top 5 budgeting tips for you to make the most of the budgeting exercise:

1. Track Your Expenses Daily

I already said this, but it is worth repeating: if you track your expenses daily, there is less room for error. Trying to remember a week later what expenses you have had can be frustrating and demotivating. You can avoid this trap by budgeting daily. Remember: only if your budgeting sheet is correct can you draw valid conclusions from it and take corrective action.

Further, budgeting daily keeps you much closer to the numbers. You will spot potential problem areas much quicker and can move faster to make adjustments.

2. Don't Give Up

In order for a budget to make sense and make a positive impact on your life and your finances, you have to stick to it. Don't give up because you get bored, or because you "forget". There is nothing to "forget" about making a budget. Look at the bigger picture: you are regaining control over your finances, which means you are regaining control over your life.

It doesn't make any sense to budget in the first week of the month, then neglect it in the second week, and then return to the Excel sheet in the following week. Be serious about it. Consistency is key. You are learning a new skill here, so cut yourself some slack for trying to improve your finances, even if it is hard at the beginning. Budgeting will become second nature after a while so don't give up!

3. Budgeting Is a Learning Experience

Budgeting is not an exam, and you are not getting graded for how well you are doing. That being said, though, budgeting is nonetheless an incredible learning experience. And believe me, learn you will. Don't beat up on yourself when you make a mistake or in case you overspend once in a while. Instead, congratulate yourself on taking action to improve your financial situation.

4. Try to Understand Your Spending Behavior

Having an open mind and being willing to learn from past mistakes is essential in order to get the most out of budgeting. Keep in mind what the core function of the budgeting process is: to raise your level of awareness of how you are spending your money! Your budgeting sheet and the associated cash flows will tell you more about yourself than you at times might want to admit. It contains the undiluted truth about your financial situation and what your real priorities in life are.

Are you honest enough with yourself when you take a hard look in the mirror?

5. Budgeting Is Empowering

Budgeting is incredibly empowering. It provides a rock-solid foundation for you to create long-term wealth and helps you keep track of your savings goals. Budgeting will raise your financial IQ. In fact, once you get the knack of it, I wouldn't be surprised if you become a real budgeting nerd.

Recommended Budget Allocations

Budget allocations are the answer to a central question when it comes to managing and allocating your household money: how much of your income should you spend on different expense categories such as rent, utilities, food, transportation, and entertainment?

The following percentage allocations are guidelines only and your personal mileage may vary depending on the size of your family/household and whether you live in an expensive city or not.

Here's an overview of how much of your income you should spend on the following expense categories:

Housing: 30-35%

Transportation: 15-20%

Food: 10-20%

Debt payments: 5-15%

Discretionary expenses: 5-10%

Utilities: 5%

Clothing: 3-5%

Medical: 3%

Savings: 5-10%

These are just guidelines, but they can nonetheless give you a pretty good idea about whether you are overspending on some categories or not. Say, for instance, that after doing your budget for a month or two you realize that you regularly spend 20% of your income on discretionary expenses (these are your "wants" we discussed earlier), instead of 5-10%, which would be more appropriate.

Spending twice as much money as recommended on some expense categories can be justified under certain circumstances (medical bills, emergencies etc.), but that is typically not the case for discretionary expenses. You should be able to spot such deviations, ask yourself why those have occurred, and take corrective action.

If you want to push these conventionally accepted spending guidelines a bit, feel free to do so. As I have said in the last chapter, you want to save as much money as possible and pay off your debt as quickly as possible. If you have to, move back in with your parents or other family members to save rental expenses and cut transportation costs by using public transport options.

If you are single and only have a moderate amount of debt to repay, I actually recommend the following budget allocations (if you don't have any debt, put the money budgeted for debt repayments in the example below into your savings account):

Housing: 25%

Transportation: 10%

Food: 10-15%

Debt payments: Up to 20%

Discretionary expenses: 5-10%

Utilities: 5%

Clothing: 3-5%

Medical: 3%

Savings: 15-20%

My Personal Budget

Just for fun, I will give you my personal budget allocations from last month for purposes of comparison. These are the exact numbers I pulled out of last month's Excel sheet that I recommended you to use:

Housing: 15%

Transportation: 5%

Food: 12%

Debt payments: 0%

Discretionary expenses: 8%

Utilities: 4%

Clothing: 2%

Medical: 2%

Savings: 52%

As you can see, I am still an aggressive saver. I am a big believer in the "paying myself first principle" which I discussed at length in the second chapter, and I have seen for myself how much of a life-changer saving and budgeting money really is. I guess once you get into the habit of saving money and you actually see how far you can go, you are always going to be a budgeting nerd and try to avoid wasting money!

Ideally, you set your savings rate before you start the budgeting process. Say, for instance, that you get your pay from your employer on the last day of each month. I highly recommended in Chapter 2 that you pay yourself first and deposit at least 10% of your income right away into a dedicated savings, investment or retirement account. Remember the key principle when it comes to saving money and creating long-term wealth: *you want to spend what is left after saving, and not save what is left after spending.*

Making Budget Adjustments

As you budget your income and expenditures you will find that some expenses are more easily controlled than others. You may consistently spend more money on groceries than you planned for, but on the other hand may also underspend, say, on transportation.

Budgeting is an ongoing process and you might have to adjust how much money you allocate to each expense category going forward. If you continuously overspend on groceries, you need to ask yourself whether you are lacking self-discipline in sticking to your budget or whether you are just setting the allocation for groceries too low.

As such, budgeting requires you to constantly question your spending behavior, which is first and foremost an awareness exercise. As you get up to speed with my budgeting sheet, or your own customized budgeting sheet for that matter, you should find it relatively easy to make adjustments.

Are You Up for a Budgeting Challenge?

A good way to kick things into gear is to challenge and push yourself when it comes to your budgeting and savings goals.

Thus, I am challenging you to gain control over your finances and start budgeting and saving money immediately. Here's your challenge:

1) As soon as you get your next paycheck, you will start to save 10% of your income right away.

2) Download my free *Budgeting Made Simple* template.

3) Starting today, you will track every single dollar you spend for the next thirty days. It doesn't matter how little you spend. If you spend a dollar for a snack at the gas station, you will write the dollar amount

in your budgeting sheet at the end of the day. Keep track of every dollar you bring in and every dollar you spend for a month. At the end of each week, look at the budgeting sheet and the sums that are calculated automatically. Do this for *just one month*!

4)   Explain to yourself and to your family what you have learned about your financial situation.

5)   Make sure to let me know how your life has improved after completing this challenge!

If you have any questions about budgeting, or if you are struggling with a particular issue about saving money, I am happy to help. Don't hesitate to get in touch: chris@retiredby35.com, or DM me on Instagram (retiredby35) or YouTube (retiredby35).

Key Takeaways

● A budget is a plan that helps you manage your money and achieve your financial goals. It structures your finances and educates you about your weaknesses;

● Use a budget regularly, keep it current and free of mistakes;

● Be serious about budgeting and actually do the work. Download my free *Budgeting Made Simple* template from my website www.retiredby35.com and get on top of your financial situation;

● Identify savings potential by questioning your spending;

● For most people, housing, transportation and food expenses are the biggest expense categories, and have the largest savings potential;

● Use the spending guidelines in this chapter to determine whether or not you are overspending;

● Adjust your budget as necessary;

● Accept my budgeting challenge and (re)gain control over your finances and your life.

CHAPTER 4

TACKLING DEBT

"A man in debt is so far a slave."

~ *Ralph Waldo Emerson*

F inancial Freedom 101: Debt is bad. Real bad. Unless, of course, you have *good* debt and not *bad* debt, which are two very different kinds of debt. Not all kinds of debts are created equal, and while one form of debt is actually desirable, the other one is a total no-no.

So, what's the difference?

Good debt is debt that is *productive.* If you use mortgage debt to buy a house or an investment property or take out a loan to expand your business, that kind of debt is typically considered to be good debt. Good debt is debt that you use to invest and make more money. If you take out a mortgage to finance the purchase of an investment property and get the tenant to repay your debt, for example, that is just smart investing. Student loan debt can be productive debt if the obtained college degree increases the market value of the student after graduation (i.e. the degree leads to a higher salary).

Bad debt, on the other hand, is debt that you use to finance impulse purchases and consumer goods that you want but don't really need. Classic examples include a more expensive car or a larger smart TV financed with debt, or designer clothes that you think you need and put on your credit card. Whatever you want to buy with it, high-interest rate consumer and credit card debt is a really, really bad thing.

Whether you like it or not, your current debt situation tells a pretty good story about you and how skillfully you deal with money. What kind of debt you have and how much you owe broadcasts to everyone around you whether you are good with money or not, and what your real priorities in life are (most people will say it is financial freedom, but it really is not!).

As a general rule, you should stay away from consumer debt as far as possible.

Debt is toxic, and it robs you of your future. There is absolutely nothing to gain from this kind of debt, except delusional short-term gratification.

A big problem in the United States when it comes to consumer and credit card debt is the easy availability of credit cards, which make it way too easy for people to make impulse buys even when they really can't afford them. According to Gallup, the average American owns 2.6 credit cards and 34% of Americans own more than that, i.e. they have at least 3 credit cards. What makes things worse is that people don't have to do anything to qualify for a credit card. Even dogs and dead people can get credit cards easily these days (not kidding!).

Easy access to credit cards combined with poor impulse control often leads to the beginning of a life-sucking debt spiral that can throw people's entire lives into chaos and financial insecurity. I alluded to this problem in Chapter 2 when I said that banks and credit card companies bank on you messing up. If you forget to make payments on time, or simply can't because you don't have the money, credit card companies and banks will happily slap more fees on you, often worth hundreds of dollars. This, of course, comes in addition to your normal interest payments on your credit card debt, which tends to have the highest interest rates of any form of debt.

The best way to avoid this problem altogether is to not use any credit cards at all! Cut up your credit cards and pay everything in cash!

Refusing to use credit cards out of principle will prevent you from giving in to temptations and making stupid decisions on a whim. It also has another side effect that will continue to support your mindset shift towards becoming more frugal and respectful of money: when you pay everything in cash, you will be much more critical about whether you actually want to buy something.

You should definitely try it.

Debt Situation in America

Americans love debt, more than anybody else in the world.

According to the Federal Reserve Bank of New York, Americans owed a total of $13.9 trillion (with a "t") at the end of the second quarter of 2019, spread out over various forms of debt. The average American household is about $136,200 in debt. The average American with a credit card owed $6,800. The average American with student loans owed $46,800, and the average auto loan debt was $27,700.

55% of Americans don't regularly pay their credit card balances in full, meaning they are carrying their balances over to the next month, and banks are very happy about this: the average APR, or annual percentage range (effectively your interest rate), exceeds 17%, and for some people with bad credit, this can easily go up to 25%.

People aged 45-54 owe the most credit card debt in the United States: $9,096 on average. As people approach regular retirement age, they become a little bit more careful with credit card debt, but not by much: people aged 65-69 still carry $6,786 credit card debt on average.

Interestingly, the more money people make, the more the average credit card balances rise. People that make $25,000 or less have approximately $3,000 in credit card debt, and people with incomes ranging from $45,000 to $70,000 owe $4,900 on their credit cards, also on average. People with very high incomes that pull in $160,000 or more annually are $11,200 in credit card debt.

That's worth repeating: people with higher incomes also have more credit card debt than folks with smaller incomes. And it makes somewhat sense. If you earn a good chunk of money every month, it is easier to deal with credit card debt, right?

But do you also remember what I told you about "lifestyle creep" earlier in this book? Lifestyle creep essentially means that your expenditures (and credit card debts) go up as your income rises because you adjust your lifestyle upwards. As a result, higher lifestyle expenses prevent you from saving money, even though you have a higher income. Lifestyle creep effects people of all income ranges, and the numbers here seem to confirm this.

How Much Debt Do You Have?

As I said at the beginning of the book, you will never have any hope of getting out of debt or improving your financial situation if you keep running away from facing the demon. In case you don't know how much money you owe, take a blank piece of paper and list all your debts. List all of your debts, credit lines, loans from friends and family, and unpaid credit card balances, and make sure you don't forget the smallest amount of debt. If you have multiple credit cards, list all unpaid balances individually. If you owe student debt, list it. Do you carry a mortgage on your primary residence? Write down how much you owe. Do you owe money for your car (I hope you don't!)? Write it down. Then calculate a sum total.

Knowing *how much* you owe is the first step towards freeing yourself from your debt burden. Now that you have taken inventory and know what and how much you have to repay, you can develop an action plan that lays out specific steps you can follow in order to reduce your debt to zero, $1 at a time.

Debt Avalanche vs. Debt Snowball

What I need you to do next is to rank your debt from highest interest rate to lowest interest rate. Whether your specific debt is small debt or large debt doesn't matter for the time being. You want to have the debt with the highest interest rate at the top of your sheet of paper, and then you should rank your debts in descending order.

The idea here is that it makes mighty economic sense for you to prioritize repaying the debt with the highest interest rate first, which is typically credit card debt. This is often referred to as the "debt avalanche method," which means you are making minimum payments on all debts as contractually required, and using excess funds to repay the debt with the highest interest rate.

Say, for example, that you owe $2,000 on each of your three credit cards and that you pay a 15% interest rate on each of them. Let us also assume that you owe $50,000 on your mortgage at 3%, and $8,000 on your car at 5%.

Instead of tackling the largest debt first, your mortgage, you should repay the outstanding balances on your debts with the highest interest rates, your credit cards, first.

As such, you would want to aggressively attack the $6,000 combined credit card debt. If those credit cards themselves differ in terms of APR, you would want to first repay the outstanding balance on the credit card with the highest APR. After you have cleared out the most expensive debt, you should focus on eating away at that 5%-interest auto loan, and only then focus on putting excess funds towards retiring your mortgage debt.

A lot of people want to start to repay the smallest debts first, as the cancellation of this debt works as motivation and gives them a sense of accomplishment. This method is often referred to as the "debt snowball method", which means you are paying the smallest debt off first and work your way up to larger debts without taking their interest rates into consideration.

I do **not** recommend this method, because it solely appeals to emotion. Economic sense dictates that you repay the debt with the highest interest rate first. This approach, though it may not make you feel as accomplished as the snowball method, will save you real money over time. Always repay the most expensive debt first!

Valuable Resources If You Struggle With Debt

Remember what I said in the last chapter when we discussed budgeting strategies that can help you get a grip on your finances? A budget is a plan, first and foremost. Without a plan you are floating around life like a captain-less container ship on the ocean. And if you have no direction, you are just lost. Obviously, the same is true when it comes to tackling your debt situation. In order to create a lasting solution to your - temporary - debt problems, it is paramount to recognize what got you into your debt situation in the first place.

If you have got student loan or mortgage debt - mostly productive debt -, you just have to eat away at your debt balance with persistence and stoicism over time. If, on the other hand, you have accumulated credit card debt because you can't resist making impulse purchases and your credit card is the only financial lifeline you have to make ends meet, you have to carefully and honestly scrutinize your spending behavior.

Recognizing that you are not doing great with money is nothing to be ashamed about. I can tell you that I made all the money mistakes one could ever hope to make myself, and most of them twice. The path towards financial freedom starts with recognizing that *you* are responsible for your financial situation. If you are staring at a big chunk of consumer debt right now, you probably have only yourself to blame. As much as it may hurt, it is the truth. However, as long as you are willing to take responsibility for your spending and adjust your behavior, you can improve your financial situation over time.

Since you have now listed all of your debts and ranked them based on their interest rates, it is time to concentrate on repaying your debt with the highest interest rate. Eat away at your debt balances $1 at a time and use the savings and budgeting guidelines from the previous two chapters to help you navigate your finances. This process may take time and may suck over the short haul, but there is no way out other than sucking it up and putting as much money as you can possibly afford towards retiring your existing debts.

Of course, if you feel overwhelmed by the task of sorting out your debt situation, there are plenty of resources out there that can help you untangle your finances.

One great resource I would like to share with you is the website of the Consumer Financial Protection Bureau, or CFPB, which is a U.S. government agency tasked with overseeing the financial sector. Specifically, the Consumer Financial Protection Bureau was created under the Dodd-Frank Wall Street Reform and Consumer Protection Act after the financial crisis of 2007/8, and the bureau is tasked primarily with protecting consumers from predatory lending practices.

The website of the CFPB is www.consumerfinance.gov and contains lots of useful information that you can use - in addition to the advice provided in this book - to tackle your debt challenges. The Consumer Financial Protection Bureau also provides a pathway for consumers to submit a complaint about financial institutions and educates the public about matters such as debt collection, debt consolidation, and understanding credit reports.

Another valuable resource I would like to share with you is the National Foundation for Credit Counseling, or NFCC. According to the foundation's website:

"The National Foundation for Credit Counseling, founded in 1951, is the nation's largest and longest-serving nonprofit financial counseling organization. The NFCC's mission is to promote the national agenda for financially responsible behavior, and build capacity for its members to deliver the highest-quality financial education and counseling services."

The National Foundation for Credit Counseling offers counseling with respect to bankruptcies, credit card debt, and foreclosures, and also helps to develop debt management plans. The website is www.nfcc.org and contains a host of valuable information that you might want to check out.

Contacting the CFPB or NFCC are good and advisable first steps to take when you are in debt and are seeking a permanent solution to your financial situation. I am not a credit counselor, and people's debt situations are often hugely complicated and personal, which is why I am not going to go into more detail here.

Your Credit Score and Why It Matters

Your credit score is hugely important if you want to buy a house or car, or if you want to get a credit card. Financial institutions and other companies use credit scores - which are based on your credit report - in order to determine how likely you are to pay back a loan.

This makes a lot of sense. Financial companies and lenders risk losing money if they treat all customers the same. Some people deal with money more responsibly than others, thus, have better credit quality and lower default risk. Credit scores are a way for financial companies and lenders to assess how you have dealt with money in the past, and, based on this information, predict how likely it is that you are going to pay back your mortgage, auto loan, or credit card debt.

One particularly often used scoring method results in the so-called FICO score, which I am sure you have crossed paths with already. FICO stands for the Fair Isaac Corporation which was one of the first companies to calculate credit scores. Most financial companies today use FICO scores in order to decide whether or not to approve you for a mortgage or a car loan.

Companies that collect credit information from you are Experian, Equifax, and TransUnion. Credit scores are calculated based on differing methodologies that take into account the length of your credit history, type of debt you owe, current state of your debt, whether or not you are a new loan applicant, etc. As a result, it is not unusual at all for all three consumer credit reporting companies to calculate a different FICO score for you.

According to the Federal Trade Commission, you are entitled to one free credit report every 12 months from each of the three consumer credit reporting companies: Experian, Equifax and TransUnion, and you should get them. You can request your credit reports free of charge on the website AnnualCreditReport.com, or follow the steps outlined on the website of the Consumer Financial Protection Bureau.

What is important to understand is that it is not only banks and financial companies that take a look at your FICO score in order to assess your credit worthiness, which is something a lot of people may not have realized yet. Your credit score - which really is a score of your financial behavior - is of interest to a lot of people, especially those that may consider entering into a business or financial relationship with you.

Parties that are interested in your credit score include prospective employers, business partners, insurance companies, mobile phone companies, advertisers, or landlords. It is in your very best financial interest to keep a good credit score and, if possible, raise it.

What Is a 'Good' FICO Score?

FICO scores run from 300 to 850. Obviously, the higher your FICO score, the more favorable a bank, for instance, will view your loan or mortgage application; for example, you have a much better chance of getting a lower interest rate on your requested mortgage loan when you have a high FICO score. From the bank's point of view, a high FICO score signals a high likelihood of you being able to repay your loan.

A FICO score in the range of 670-739 is generally considered to be good while a score between 740-799 is seen as very good. A score of 800 or higher is as good as it gets, all but assuring you the most favorable credit terms. The majority of Americans, 67% (according to Experian), have a FICO score of 670 or above. 17% of Americans have a FICO score of 580-669, and 16% of Americans have very poor FICO scores ranging from 300-579. The overwhelming majority of delinquencies occurs in the 669-or-lower FICO score group.

5 Factors That Influence Your FICO Score

A couple of factors impact the calculation of your FICO score, and some have a higher weighting than others. Here's what influences your FICO score:

- Your payment history (35%);

- How much debt you owe (30%);

- The length of your credit history (15%);

- How much of your credit is new (10%);

- What types of credit you use (10%).

Your payment history is by far the most influential factor for the calculation of your credit score. The more reliable you are when it comes to making payments on time, the higher your FICO score will be, and the more trustworthy you will appear to a lender.

What Can You Do to Boost Your FICO Score?

You can do quite a few things in order to ensure that you get a high FICO score, or raise your current FICO score. The single most important thing for you to do is to *pay your bills on time.*

It never ceases to amaze me how many people don't pay their bills on time. It's mind-boggling to me. You have a bill to pay? Pay it. And pay it on time. If you are one of those people that tends to "forget" things, set reminders in your calendar a day before the bill is due, and make a conscious decision to stay on top of things.

Paying your bills is not something that you should forget. Not paying bills on time reflects poorly on you and can lead to higher costs down the road if you are pressed to pay late fees. Make it a habit to pay your bills on time. I, for instance, always have to pay my utility bill on the 4th day of each month. I never forget it. You know why? Because I made it a *habit* to pay my electric bill on every 4th day of the month. Paying your bills on time is a key skill that you need to master, especially if you are shooting for something as ambitious as financial freedom.

There are a couple of other things that you can do in order to boost your credit score. One thing is to not max out your credit line. A maxed-out credit line is a red flag for many banks and indicates poor financial management, whether that may be true in your case, or not.

Ironically, at least in United States, the longer your credit history is, the better the chances are that you will get a high FICO score. The reason is simple: the longer your track record of paying your bills and meeting your financial obligations, the higher your "trust factor". The longer you have proven that you can reliably service your debt, the lower your perceived risk is.

Paying down debt, obviously, is another way to raise your FICO score. When you repay your debts, you improve your debt-to-credit ratio which, in turn, will raise your score.

Lastly, credit reports can also be erroneous, which means you should check them regularly. A lot of data from different sources makes its way into your credit report and there are quite a few ways in which errors can find their way into your report, too. If you find errors in your credit report, the first thing you should do is to dispute the information and contact the credit reporting company that provided you with the erroneous report. Removing false information from your credit report is one of the fastest ways to boost your FICO score.

FICO Score and Financing Costs

I highlighted the distinction between productive and unproductive debt at the beginning of this chapter. To recap: productive debt is investment debt that you take on in order to gain financial benefits in the long term, for example, a mortgage loan that you use to invest in an income-producing property, or a bank loan that you use to start or expand your business.

A high FICO score, 670 or higher, will allow you to get better credit terms, i.e. a lower interest rate. High FICO scores, thus, immediately benefit your payment terms and, by extension, improve the economics of the deal you are pursuing. The higher you can push your FICO score, the better your mortgage payment terms will be, and the higher the profits will be that you can squeeze out of your rental property, for example.

If your FICO score is between 760-850, you can expect an interest rate of 3.32% for a $216,000 30-year fixed rate mortgage and a $948 monthly mortgage payment. On the other hand, if your FICO score is between 620-639, the bank will lend you money only at a much higher rate, 4.91%, for the same loan (data as of June 2019). The monthly payment will be $1,147, a whopping $199/month, or 21% more than the person with the higher FICO score needs to pay. The applicant with the better FICO score in this example will save $199/month, $2,388/year, and $71,640 over the life of the loan. That's not just small potatoes, that's really significant!

Debt is not always bad. In fact, debt - if used correctly - is a powerful force multiplier. We will explore this in greater detail in Chapter 8 when we discuss real estate investing.

Key Takeaways

- Debt robs you of your future. High-interest consumer debt is especially toxic;

- Write down all the debts you owe on one piece of paper and gain clarity over your debt situation;

- Rank your debts from highest interest rate debt to lowest interest rate debt (ignore absolute debt amounts);

- Prioritize repaying the debt with the highest interest rate and work your way down to the debt with the lowest interest rate;

- Repay your debt stoically, $1 at a time;

- Cut up your credit cards and adopt the habit of paying for everything in cash. No exceptions!

- FICO scores have a large influence over how much interest you pay on different types of debt;

- Check your credit report for accuracy and dispute inaccurate information by contacting the consumer credit reporting companies;

- Raising your FICO score is incredibly important if you want to apply for a mortgage and use real estate investing to generate wealth;

- Higher FICO scores translate into better payment terms and can potentially yield tens of thousands of dollars in savings;

- The fastest way to raise your FICO score is to pay your bills on time and repay outstanding debts as fast as possible.

CHAPTER 5

MAXIMIZING INCOME

"If you think you can do a thing or think you can't do a thing,

you're right."

~ Henry Ford

I n the preceding three chapters we have discussed minimizing your lifestyle expenses, budgeting, and getting out of debt, all of which are indispensable core strategies if you want to work slowly but steadily towards financial freedom.

That being said, I am not just advocating for reasonable frugality as an approach to financial independence. As far as I am concerned, a dual strategy that combines *minimizing expenses* with *maximizing income* is the most promising strategy to build a solid financial foundation that will set the base for your early retirement.

You can go very far in life just by saving money on a consistent basis. The financial examples provided in this book (recall the examples that calculated the future value of your car payments and your coffee addiction) provide sufficient evidence as to how powerful it is to save and invest money over long periods of time.

Maximizing income is a **complimentary** strategy that you should use **in addition** to sticking to your savings goals (including raising your savings rate over time), budgeting your expenses, and accelerating debt repayments in order to retire early.

Maximizing your income is a broad term and it includes a couple of elements that I like to divide into four distinct groups:

1. Maximizing income through hustling in your main gig/career/job;

2. Maximizing income through a side hustle;

3. Maximizing income based on investments in the stock and real estate markets;

4. Maximizing income through reinvestment of dividends and bond and real estate income.

We will discuss various options for maximizing your income as it relates to earned income (bullet points #1 and #2) in this chapter. Maximizing your income through investments in income-producing assets will be discussed in depth in Chapter 7 (stocks) and Chapter 8 (real estate), and the importance of compounding (reinvestment) will be handled in Chapter 9.

Grow Your Income by Investing in Yourself

Earned income is the money that you earn from paid work. Typically, most people have jobs or careers in which they exchange their time and labor for money. In its most simple form, an employee goes to work for his or her employer and works a set amount of hours, typically around 40 hours a week. Once a month, and in some professions once every two weeks, the employer pays the employee for his or her time and labor.

Earned income is the reality for most people, not only in the United States, but almost everywhere in the world. Unfortunately, there is one really big problem with earned income: when you stop going to work and putting in the time, the money stops as well. Understand this: as long as you depend on earned income in order to pay for your lifestyle, you will continue to have to show up to the rat race ... that is why it is so important to create **passive** income streams from stocks and real estate. Passive income is money that you earn from your investments and that requires little or no ongoing effort.

If you invest more time and effort into your education and obtain a college degree, you may qualify for higher-paid positions in the corporate world, such as an accountant, software designer, engineer, lawyer, doctor, or university professor. Due to your higher level of competence, you can now demand a higher market price for your labor.

Education still matters in the U.S. labor market. Just consider these simple statistics from the U.S. census bureau (based on 2017 numbers):

● The median annual income of workers with a high school diploma was $35,256 (5.4% unemployment rate);

● The median annual income of a worker with an associate degree was $41,496 (4.3% unemployment rate);

● The median income of a worker that earned a bachelor's degree was $59,124/year (2.8% unemployment rate);

● The median annual income of someone with a master's degree was $69,732/year (2.4% unemployment rate).

There are two takeaways here: 1. The higher your level of education, the higher your income and life-time earnings, and 2. The more educated you become, the lower the unemployment rate and the lower the risk of sliding into poverty.

So, obviously, investing in yourself pays huge dividends in America and elsewhere, despite the high costs of obtaining a college education.

The important thing here, though, is that you should choose a career that you are interested in and that you are at least mildly passionate about. If you choose a career that makes your stomach turn every morning, you are probably working in the wrong field.

I say this because more than half of Millennials choose jobs primarily because of a job's salary, status and associated perks. There is a huge danger in choosing a career based on money and status alone: you are going to spend the majority of your time in your life at work, and it is not going to be very fulfilling or good for your overall well-being if you choose a career purely because of the money.

Ideally, you should choose a career that you are both passionate about and that has attractive earnings potential. Maximizing your income will be so much easier for you if you are doing something that you actually care about. It never ceases to amaze me how few people actually do what they love. Most people you meet simply don't. So, if you take just one thing away from this chapter, it should be that maximizing your earnings will be so much easier for you if you are in a career that is aligned with your values and that piques your interests.

Obviously, the more money you make in your career, the more money you can put towards early retirement. Hence, I always recommend young people in their 20s and even 30s to hustle in their careers, try new things, take risks, seek out responsibilities, think long-term, and grow their earnings through promotions, if possible. If you combine this hustle approach to your career with a frugal approach to living (saving, budgeting, respecting money, and avoiding debt), you will be invincible and will make giant steps towards early retirement.

Of course, I do recognize that not a lot of people necessarily are lucky enough to *choose* a job or career that they are passionate about. The advice to "do something that you love" can sound a bit irritating to people that have run into some bad luck, whose finances are out of whack, are weighed down by health issues, have dependents to take care of, or live in an area where jobs are scarce. I get that.

However, with the explosion of the internet, everyone nowadays has the chance to participate in the internet economy and start a side hustle easily. So, even if your main gig is not that satisfying or financially lucrative for you right now, there is an alternative to maximizing your income: you now have the opportunity to hustle online for yourself on your free time! It doesn't matter what you look like, where you live, or how much money you have in your bank account right now. These days you can literally start a business from your bed for less than $100!

The internet is a real game-changer and a true equalizer for scores of people that feel they have been left behind or struggle to make ends meet. It provides free-thinking solopreneurs and people prepared to hustle in order to achieve financial freedom with a never-ending stream of business opportunities.

Top 10 Side Hustle Ideas for Extra Income

The internet levels the playing field and you can start a side hustle in almost anything you are passionate about. You don't have to give up your main job and jump with both feet into a big, black hole of uncertainty. A side hustle affords you with the luxury to test the water one toe at a time. Find out what works for you, and disregard what does not.

You can now open an account on a freelancer platform such as Upwork, Fiverr or Freelancer.com and offer your services to a global audience. Whether you are good at writing blog articles, editing book manuscripts, designing graphics, coding apps, building websites, managing Instagram accounts, copy-editing, or doing market research, you can now offer your service relatively effortlessly from your home office, wherever this may be.

Whatever it is that you are good at, there is a chance you can make money from it with a side hustle. A side hustle is a great way of making some extra cash, creating a (passive) income stream, and testing entrepreneurial waters before you jump "all-in".

Here are my "Top 10 Side Hustle" ideas as they have appeared the first time on my personal finance blog www.retiredby35.com:

1. Write an E-book

Writing and publishing your own e-book is a great accomplishment. Though writing and editing an entire book can be quite daunting, publishing your own book or e-book is a nice way to make some extra cash on the side while helping others out with practical advice. I myself have written numerous e-books and have gone through the process multiple times. My tip: select a niche that is related to your passion and research what topics readers are interested in. Invest time into writing a quality e-book, get it published on Amazon.com, and don't forget the marketing!

2. Start Your Own Blog

This one is a classic. Starting a blog is a nice way of building an audience and sharing valuable information with them. Start a blog about something that you are passionate about, a hobby, or something that you like to do when you have free time. Blogs can be monetized through affiliate marketing links, ads, and by selling your own product.

3. Create a Course on Udemy

Everybody has a skill that can be monetized. If you are good at coding websites, designing book covers, or digital marketing, create a course that teaches people how to do those things. You can sell those courses on online learning platforms such as Udemy or Skillshare. The more valuable your content, the more people will sign up for your course, the more money you are going to make from course sales!

4.   Start an Amazon FBA Business

Amazon has morphed into a giant e-commerce platform that provides enterprising individuals with an endless stream of opportunities to sell everything from iPhone accessories to scented candles.

Amazon FBA, which stands for *Fulfilled by Amazon,* is an attractive option for side-hustling digital entrepreneurs who want to sell their products to a large customer base. In the past, niche products such as bracelets, earrings, or yoga mats have been successful items to sell on Amazon. Once you have shipped your products to an Amazon warehouse, you will need to drive traffic to your Amazon product page and get people to buy your stuff, which arguably is the main challenge here.

The benefit of Amazon FBA is that the e-commerce retailer handles the entire sales process. The shortcoming, however, is that securing a high ranking on Amazon is not an easy feat. Plus, with Amazon FBA, you need to invest money into inventory first.

5.   Start a Drop Shipping Business

Drop shipping is very similar to Amazon FBA. All you need to do is select some products you want to sell and create your own online store via Etsy or Shopify. When customers buy a product from your online store, you place an identical order with your supplier from Aliexpress, for example, and have him ship the order directly to your customers. The beauty is, you don't have to invest any money into building an inventory. On the other hand, you have to spend money on ads to drive traffic to your store and drop shipping has become harder lately due to the fact that so many people are doing it. My tip: pick a trendy niche product that has proven to sell, and make sure you pick a reliable supplier with a decent number of positive reviews (50+) from Aliexpress. Setting up a drop shipping store costs as little as a couple hundred bucks.

6. Sell Your Skills on Fiverr

Are you good at SEO, graphic design, or formatting documents? Then head over to freelancer platforms such as Fiverr.com where you can offer your services to customers worldwide and start making money today.

7. Teach Languages Online

If you are a native English speaker, there is a good chance that you can teach English online to students in Asia, mainly China. Try websites such as www.dadaabc.com or www.vipkidteachers.com and submit your application. These online language teaching companies tend to pay hourly rates of $14 or more, which is competitive compared to what many U.S.-based part-time jobs pay. If you are not a native English speaker, there is also room to teach other languages. If you speak Spanish, French, Italian or German, you can try and teach on www.italki.com for an average hourly rate of $20-$25 (before commissions).

8.   Create an App

If you are into coding and understand software development, creating an app might be another opportunity for you to start a side hustle and make some extra money. Find a niche and code an app that solves people's problems. Think of productivity, health, fitness, dieting, or investment apps. The market is crowded for sure, but there is always an opening in the market for somebody that creates value.

9.   Retail Arbitrage

When you engage in retail arbitrage you buy a product from a large retailer such as Walmart and then immediately flip it for a higher price on another e-Commerce platform like Amazon.com or eBay.com. Lots of people are making a good amount of money with it.

10. Create a Subscription Business

This one is probably the most time-consuming and labor-intensive side hustle idea on this list. However, you can make a LOT of money with it. A subscription business is attractive, first and foremost, because of its recurring income. If you are good at something and you can create a community around it, people are willing to pay for your digital or physical products and your coaching and guidance. If you are, for example, a fitness nut and interested in nutrition and health, you can build your own personal brand and sell meal plans, training manuals, and 1-on-1 coaching sessions.

As you can see, there is no shortage of opportunities to start a side hustle today, and with the development of new technologies in the future, there will be even more opportunities coming your way tomorrow. Starting a side hustle is a great way of making some extra cash, creating passive income and exploring your passions. More importantly, you never know where your side hustle will take you. Maybe you will even be able to leave the corporate rat race behind entirely once you start exploring the exciting world of online businesses and find a niche that works for you.

The Art of the Hustle: How I Saved and Invested $50,000 While Still In High School

Whether you are working in your main gig or trying out a side gig, the main focus is on *hustling*. If you are in your 20s or 30s, hustle as much as possible and try to learn as much as possible. Fail early, fail hard, but fail forward and learn to shrug off failure without taking it personally. Confidence and ignorance go a long way together and they can lead to incredible success.

The best thing you can do in order to maximize your income, and I can't emphasize this enough, is to develop an excellent work ethic. Your work attitude will be the number one driver of success and earnings in your professional life. The beauty about having a great work attitude is that it doesn't cost you anything and that it allows you to gain a significant competitive advantage over your peers, even those that are seemingly smarter than you.

In order to develop a fantastic work attitude, try to make a point out of the following suggestions:

- Always be on time.

- Show up early.

- Dress to impress.

- Have a can-do attitude.

- Accept challenges.

- Never be intimidated, not by your competition and not by your challenge.

- *Always* put your customers and clients first.

- Be honest, and reward honesty.

- Always under-promise and over-deliver.

- Be kind and friendly to everyone, especially people that are **not** your superiors.

- Accept negative feedback, but don't take it personal.

- Use a firm handshake and confident body language.

- When angry, do not speak.

- Always volunteer for extra hours and extra assignments.

- Go the extra mile.

A good work attitude goes a really long way, and it shines through in everything you do. All of the behaviors listed above are important. If you are prepared to go the extra mile, your earnings will grow very quickly.

When I worked in Australia for a wedding event company, I made a habit out of volunteering for extra shifts. When I just started to work for this company, my supervisor would come to me and ask if I could work on Saturday or Sunday night. Before he would even be able to tell me where I had to go and what the specific job was, I would interrupt him with an enthusiastic, "Yes, of course." I could tell by my supervisor's reaction that he was irritated at my response because I didn't even give him the time to tell me specifics.

And that was because I did not care! You see, my attitude was that I would volunteer for every shift and every extra job available. I didn't care at all where I had to go and when the job started, or how I would get there. I just knew I would figure it out. I always did. I did every job I could get my hands on: I worked at 5 a.m. on Sundays, I worked until midnight on Fridays (when everyone I knew was out partying), I volunteered for shifts that started on Saturday night at 2 a.m. I volunteered for jobs 3 hours away from my company's headquarters. I volunteered for everything!

As you can imagine, I quickly developed a reputation in my company for my positive work attitude. My supervisor stopped asking me about whether I wanted extra jobs, and just assigned them to me, which was exactly the way I liked it. Extra shifts and overtime pay started to flow to me naturally. Competition was usually very low for extra shifts, which made it so much easier for me to make bank.

I had weekends where I worked 36 hours in two days, and weeks where I worked close to 100 hours, and I was on the job 7 days a week. I made my job my absolute priority, which is also why I earned 30-40% more each month than my peers in the same job. I really hustled, and it really paid off, literally: In my first six months on the job I saved more than $30,000!

This was not the first time that I hustled, though. I hustled from an early age on, and I saved most of the money that I made.

I remember when I was fourteen and worked a whole range of odd jobs in order to bring in some cash. During summer school holidays, for instance, I worked 5-6 hours in the morning in a gardening company before cycling 3 miles on my shitty bike, uphill for the most part, to do a paper route that paid me $20-$25 for my 3-hour run. Do you know what I did with all the money I earned? I saved it!

My friends couldn't wrap their heads around it. They also had some part-time jobs but blew their entire summer earnings on new gaming computers. When school started again after the summer break, they had the latest computers but they were usually broke again, too. I never had (nor did I need) the newest computers and latest gadgets in order to feel happy or fulfilled. My satisfaction came from seeing my savings build up month after month. I did this sort of thing for 4 years, taking odd jobs as a high school student whenever I could. At the end of high school, I had saved up the equivalent of $50,000.

Here are a couple of things I did to make bank:

● I delivered newspapers when it was brutally hot and when it rained and snowed;

● I delivered promotional materials for a bathroom contractor on my bicycle to newly constructed houses during cold and snowy winters;

● I sold used books at flea markets;

● I worked on construction sites doing hard labor, digging dirt, lifting steel bars, and cleaning up stuff;

● I mowed lawns;

● I helped construct fences;

● I sold my Dad's used computer magazines to classmates in high school;

● I bought and sold second-hand computer games;

● I sold computer parts;

● I tried to sell new laptop computers (my first business, which failed miserably);

● I wrote product reviews online for money;

● I tutored students in Math and English;

I did all of these things before I was 18 years old.

I was always a freak, and I saved the overwhelming portion of the money I earned in those odd jobs. It is quite funny, actually, looking back and realizing how much I was willing to suffer in terrible jobs for an average pay of maybe $3-$5/hour as a teenager. But without a shadow of a doubt, the hustle in my teenage years paid big dividends and definitely set the financial foundation for my early retirement. It also instilled a great work ethic in me.

The key takeaway here is this: saving small amounts of money consistently *plus* hustling and looking for additional income sources is an unbeatable combination, and it puts you on the fast-track to financial freedom. The person that can persist and overcome peer pressure is going to be the winner and early retiree here. Just by hustling and saving seemingly insignificant amounts of money, you can give your entire life a new direction, and once you are cashed up, you can choose to take a swing whenever a business opportunity reveals itself. The downside is zero, the upside is unlimited.

Key Takeaways

- Invest in yourself and your education. This will have the largest impact on your income potential;

- In order to maximize your income, you better pick a career that you have a natural interest in and that you are passionate about;

- If you have no flexibility in leaving your main gig right now, look for a side hustle. Choose one that centers around your hobbies, passions, and intrinsic interests. A good starting point is the side hustle list I provided in this chapter;

- Side hustles often have no downside at all but have the potential to really take off if you dedicate enough time to them. Side hustles can grow into main hustles fairly easily;

- Hustle as much as you can and take as many risks as possible as long as you are young;

- A can-do work attitude will get you very far in life and costs you absolutely nothing. My income exploded as soon as I embraced inconvenience and did the work others didn't want to do;

- Going the extra mile is very powerful because most people are not prepared to do it. Going the extra mile and putting in the extra effort is what will get you noticed;

- Volunteer for extra shifts (and extra pay) at any opportunity.

CHAPTER 6

FUNDAMENTALS OF INVESTING

"Knowledge is like a garden: if it's not cultivated, it cannot be harvested."

~ African Proverb

This is probably the most serious chapter of the entire book. Investing money is key to creating wealth long-term, and you definitely need to do it in order to become financially independent. Minimizing expenses and maximizing income are a dual strategy that should be used to together. Investing your savings is the next logical step that will help you greatly in achieving financial freedom.

Once you have gotten used to making a budget, and saving money has become second nature, the question ultimately becomes: "What are you going to do with the money that you set aside every month?"

If you followed my advice in Chapter 2, you are automatically putting at least 10% of your monthly income into a dedicated savings account. While saving 10% or more of your paycheck is worthy of applause, savings accounts generally offer savers pitiful returns. In some parts of the world, like in Europe, negative interest rates prevail today, meaning savers have to pay the bank to deposit money with them.

The problem resulting from low-yielding savings accounts is magnified due to the fact that inflation hurts your savings over time. Inflation is an important consideration for both savers and investors. The standard savings account in the United States currently yields less than 1%. The long-term inflation rate, however, is closer to 2%, which is a problem for one particular reason: your real purchasing power decreases over time.

Let me explain.

Say, for instance, that you rent an apartment in your hometown and that a provision in your rental contract stipulates that your rent automatically increases every year by 2%. If your income doesn't go up by 2% every year also, you end up spending a larger percentage of your income on your rent. In other words, your *real* purchasing power decreases as your cost of living goes up.

Libraries around the world are filled with economic text books that illustrate the corrosive effect inflation has on wealth because it has huge implications for everyone: workers, banks, insurance companies, investment firms, and, of course, investors.

Since inflation decreases your purchasing power over time, you need to earn an investment return that, over the long-term, beats the inflation rate. If we were to assume that the long-term annual inflation rate stays around 2%, you need to earn an investment return with your stock and real estate portfolio of at least 2%. The goods news is that there are plenty of investment vehicles out there - stocks, bonds, funds, and investment properties - that fit this bill. The long-term return on stocks (depending on who you consult), is between 7 and 10%. This means that if you invested in a diversified portfolio of stocks, you can reasonably expect to earn a total return of between 7 and 10% annually going forward. Total returns consist of dividend income and capital appreciation.

I should note here, in order to avoid confusion later on, that the 7 to 10% total annual investment return mentioned here relates to long-term average stock returns. Stock markets, just like the economy, move in cycles, which means that periods of strong economic growth are followed by economic contractions. Thus, stock market returns can fluctuate wildly from year to year as well, and it is not uncommon for stock prices to retreat 20% or more in a single year. Over the long run, however, stocks and real estate produce total returns in the high single digits. Of course, your own ambition, timing skill, and risk tolerance will have an extraordinary influence on your final investment results.

Should you have already succeeded in building up some savings, now is the time to take the next step on your journey towards financial independence:

You actually have to start to invest your money for higher returns. How you are going to do this and where you need to start is what we are going to discuss next.

4-Step Investment Process

Investing money into stocks or real estate may sound a bit scary at first, especially if you are a new to investing, but trust me, you will be fine. Investing is actually pretty straightforward and always follows the same basic 4-step process which we will explore throughout this and the next chapter:

1. Generate your own investment ideas;

2. Assess whether or not an investment supports your goal of early retirement (provides passive income);

3. Evaluate your potential investment based on objective investment criteria, such as the investment's cash flow, earnings and valuation;

4. Actually follow through and make the investment.

It all sounds a lot harder than it is. So, without further ado, let's first discuss bullet point #1: coming up with an actionable idea.

How to Generate Your Own Investment Ideas

Generating investment ideas is very simple. If you don't have any experience in investing yet, don't worry. Just start by picking up a financial magazine every once in a while that discusses the stock market and financial events. There are lots of resources on the web that can help you guide you through the often confusing investment world. Resources that I recommend and that I use myself include a wide array of financial publications including:

- The Economist
- Fortune Magazine
- Forbes
- Kiplinger
- The Street
- Fox Business
- CNBC

You don't need to be an investment professional to understand what's going on here. Even beginner investors can learn a lot from these resources, if only they care enough to read them regularly. Reading news magazines and following events in the stock market will naturally increase your financial IQ, and, most importantly, teach you the language of finance. Once you immerse yourself in the subject of investing, you will inevitably come up with your own investment ideas, too.

I suggest you read financial news critically and always ask yourself questions that will enhance your understanding of the capital markets and that will make you a better investor in the long-term.

Questions you can ask yourself to further your understanding of the financial world include:

- What does Apple's announcement of a new streaming service mean for the company's revenues?

- How are Facebook's privacy issues going to affect the company's revenue trend?

- Should I buy Facebook's or Apple's stock now that their stocks have fallen 20% from their 52-week highs?

- Will Facebook be able to monetize Instagram, and, if so, to what extent?

- Does it make sense for ExxonMobil to buy an alternative energy company?

- Can Uber become profitable?

- Should I buy Lyft shares at an inflated valuation after the company's IPO?

- When is Airbnb going to go public, and should I buy stock?

- Will Tesla be able to dominate the self-driving car market?

- What companies are going to be profitable even if the U.S. economy goes into a recession?

- What companies are likely going to grow their dividends going forward, even when the U.S. economy grows more slowly?

- What stock has the highest dividend yield in the S&P 500, and can the company sustain its payout?

- Why does it make sense for companies to buy back stock?

- Can Netflix continue to add international subscribers in the future, and what will this likely mean for the stock price?

- What companies is Warren Buffett trying to acquire and why?

These are just some questions that you can ask yourself in order to deepen your knowledge and understanding of the financial world and learn to think for yourself. In the stock market, you can be totally right one day, and then be totally wrong the next day. I, for instance, bought Facebook stock in May 2018 *after* the Cambridge Analytica privacy scandal hit the company and I thought I was getting a good deal at $160. The stock subsequently climbed as high as $218 before plummeting when the tech company issued a revenue warning in the third quarter of 2018. On the day of the revenue warning, Facebook's stock plunged 20%, and the tech company lost a combined $119 billion in market value, which was the largest one-day drop in history. The stock dropped below $130 in the coming months. So, the question is: was I right or wrong?

Well, that depends on *when* you would have asked the question. I first bought Facebook at $160 and appeared to be right when the stock was at $218. I looked wrong, however, when the stock price dropped all the way down to $123. I really doubled down on Facebook at $140 when Facebook's stock was widely out-of-favor. You see, in the stock market you can be both right and wrong with the same investment at different times. At the time of writing, Facebook's stock has recovered and sits near $200 once again.

The point is not in being right or wrong on any single day, but in developing your own ideas about certain stocks. Facebook is by far the most efficient advertising platform on the internet, there is simply nobody that comes even close to the tech company in terms of scale. As long as advertisers love Facebook, I figured, the tech company will continue to make lots of money, privacy concerns aside. Plus, people always say they care about privacy, but they really don't. Buying Facebook at $160 and later at $140 was a no-brainer for me, and I wouldn't have bought the stock if I hadn't read about the privacy scandal in the news.

A good starting point for generating your own investment ideas is to think about companies whose products you already like. As a matter of fact, this is a rather excellent start to generating investment ideas; if you like a company's products, chances are you will know a thing or two about them.

Say, for example, you are a fan of Apple's products such as the iPhone or iPad. If you use Apple's products enthusiastically, you will likely have an informed opinion as to why you think Apple's products are superior to Samsung's products, for example. If you like Apple's innovations and the company launches its own streaming service, you will likely be in a position to judge whether the new service offering will be competitive or not.

If you like disruptive companies that put a new spin on things and that have found a way to enhance the customer experience, would you be interested in not only using their services, but buying their stocks, too? Would you be interested in buying Uber's or Lyft's stock as opposed to just using their ride sharing services? Have you used Airbnb lately on a vacation? If the experience was good and you see more and more people using Airbnb services in your social circle, would it make sense to buy shares after Airbnb listed its shares on the stock exchange? Are you a Facebook fan and impressed by their industry-leading conversion rates? Could you make an investment case for Facebook's stock here?

These, again, are just some ideas and examples of questions that you can ask yourself in order to generate your own investment ideas. There are lots of gurus out there that offer you investment and trading tips for monthly subscriptions, but all of this is totally unnecessary... if you only trusted yourself enough to use your own brain. The best investment ideas, in my opinion, are often the simplest ones.

Here is a little thought experiment that I would like you to do in order to nurture your investor mindset:

Think about **one** product that you really love and that you use passionately, and think about **one** restaurant that you can't wait to visit again. Chances are you can build an investment case around your answers: what company is producing the product you love, and what company owns the restaurant (chain) whose food you adore? Are these public companies whose stocks you could buy?

The next step would be to head over to the company's investor relations website (Google it) and just familiarize yourself a little bit with the company. Most companies have up-to-date investor presentations on their websites that you can read, which often is a hugely enlightening exercise. Investor presentations are a good tool to use because companies condense their financial information in such a way that it is easily digestible. Scrolling through an investor presentation is a great way to learn more about a company you already like. Investor presentations typically contain just the gist of the investment thesis without the level of detail you would expect from quarterly or annual reports.

If you still think that going through investor expectations or reading financial news is a too daunting and time-consuming exercise, no worries, there are other strategies for you to start investing.

One such strategy is to simply pay attention to what stocks the most successful investors in the world buy.

Learn from the Best

There are lots of investors out there that have gained investment world superstar status by consistently logging superior investment results. Some of these people are company founders, some are investment and fund managers, while others simply are investors or venture capitalists. Whatever their professions and core skills are, you can learn a lot from these investors about how they think and evaluate investments.

By far the most impressive investor, as far as I am concerned, is Warren Buffett, founder of Berkshire Hathaway. Warren Buffett is a multi-billionaire with a net worth of $84 billion in 2019, which makes him the third richest person in the world behind #1 Jeff Bezos (founder of e-Commerce giant Amazon), with a net worth of $114 billion, and #2 Bill Gates (founder of software company Microsoft), with a net worth of $105 billion. Warren Buffett managed to accumulate unfathomable wealth through his investment vehicle Berkshire Hathaway, a diversified conglomerate that invests in everything ranging from insurance companies to candy. If you invested $1,000 with Warren Buffett in 1964, at the beginning of his investment career, you would have been able to buy 52 shares for $19. Those shares are now worth $16.7 million, based on Berkshire Hathaway's stock price of $320,850 on September 13, 2019.

Of course, this investment opportunity is gone and we can't travel back to 1964 and make an investment in the past. What we can do, however, is to try to learn from Warren Buffett and soak up the investment wisdom he so freely shares at any opportunity. There is nothing more exciting than being able to watch over the shoulder of a billionaire and get some insight into how he thinks about various investments.

Warren Buffett, in particular, is a national treasure and an incredible source of investing wisdom and emotional intelligence. Warren Buffett and Charlie Munger, his long-time associate, have attained legendary status in the investor world. Thousands of shareholders and investors flock to Berkshire Hathaway's shareholder meetings in Omaha, Nebraska every year to hear Warren Buffett's thoughts on his investments and the state of the capital markets. Berkshire Hathaway's annual shareholder letter is also a fantastic resource that offers investors a peek into the thinking of the world's greatest investor.

Warren Buffett himself learned investing from Benjamin Graham, who was the author of *The Intelligent Investor*. Benjamin Graham is regarded as the father of value investing and mentored Warren Buffett at the University of Columbia. Buffett attended Columbia University after his application was rejected by Harvard University, and he ultimately graduated with a Master of Science in Economics from Columbia in 1951, after which he started out in the investment world.

Warren Buffett himself credits his investment success to the education received by Benjamin Graham and, specifically, the book *The Intelligent Investor*, which I highly recommend you to read if you are serious about gaining a deep, contextual understanding of stock market investments. The book covers everything from valuing securities to reading financial statements, and also discusses how our emotions often hurt rational investment decision-making.

Learning from the best and paying attention to sophisticated investors with outstanding performance records is a great way of coming up with investment ideas. Reading Berkshire Hathaway's annual shareholder letter won't take more than an hour or two, but you will be a lot smarter for it. If you follow the daily financial news, you will also know when Warren Buffett or his investment company Berkshire Hathaway buy stocks.

This doesn't mean, of course, that you should just blindly follow Warren Buffett and buy whatever he buys. Rather, asking yourself why Warren Buffett is acquiring another company or buying a certain stock can give you crucial insight into how to think about an investment.

For example, Warren Buffett invested billions of dollars in Goldman Sachs and Bank of America, two beleaguered Wall Street banks weighed down by billions of toxic mortgage assets, in 2008 and 2011. Banks were doing extremely poorly after the sub-prime mortgage crisis hit in 2007/8 and they threatened to drag the United States into an economic depression. While most investors did not want to touch U.S. banks with a ten-foot pole at the time (due to staggering losses, increasing regulatory oversight, public outrage and taxpayer-funded bailouts), Warren Buffett bought bank stocks when nobody else did. When the financial sector rebounded and financial stocks returned from the ashes during the subsequent economic upswing, Buffett made billions of profits on his contrarian investments. The $5 billion preferred stock investment in Goldman Sachs alone netted him a profit of $3.7 billion. At the time of writing, Berkshire Hathaway still owns his Bank of America shares, and the billionaire is set to reap many more billions of dollars in profits on this position.

There Is Never a Shortage of Investment Opportunities

Thankfully, there is never a shortage of investment opportunities in either the stock market or the real estate market. Opportunities always exist, especially when the economy cools off and asset prices decrease. Recessions have historically been good periods to buy stocks and real estate because they are cyclical investments.

Cyclical investments do well when the economy does well, just think of hotels, oil companies, airlines, or banks. In an economic upswing people have good jobs, the labor market is tight, and people and businesses are willing to spend and invest money, thanks to a high degree of confidence in the economy. As people feel more secure about their financial future, they are spending money more freely. Companies, also buoyed by a rising economy, invest in expansion and banks make more personal and commercial loans, which help them earn more interest income.

As economic growth starts to slow, this trend reverses. Companies that tend to do well during an economic upswing are also companies that don't do so well as the economy contracts. When a U.S. recession hits, lots of investors turn to more defensive stocks. Defensive stocks are stocks of companies whose earnings and cash flows are not that much affected by a cyclical downturn. Think about industries such as consumer goods, telecommunications and health care. People are going to use the services of those companies regardless of how the economy is doing.

The point here is that there is never really a time when there are no investment opportunities. The best time to buy either stocks or real estate is when the markets are in distress and investors like to stay away from risk assets. While the financial crisis of 2007/8 was bad at the time, and negatively affected millions of people that bought homes from 2004 until 2007, open-minded investors like Warren Buffett made a killing in the aftermath.

Long-Term Stock Returns

Scores of academics, financial analysts, and professional investors have studied what long-term returns investors can expect when investing in the stock market or a fund that closely resembles a major stock market index, such as the S&P 500. Results often vary because analysts use different time periods for their studies, which can have a dramatic effect on the calculated average stock market return. If you bought stocks, for example, at the peak of the dot-com bubble in the late 90s, your average annual return over the following decade was lower than the average annual return of an investor that started to invest during the following recession when stocks were seriously underpriced.

From 1926 to 2018, for example, the S&P 500 had an annual average return of approximately 10%. The longer you invest, the more likely you are to achieve higher capital returns, due to the fact that time helps investors ride out the highs and lows of the stock market.

Other studies put the long-term average annual return in the stock market at between 7 and 10%, which is still pretty good, especially in today's environment of ultra-low interest rates. In Europe, at the time of writing, there are even negative interest rates, meaning *you* have to pay the bank to take your money. Negative deposit rates are driven by a monetary policy that seeks to discourage saving and encourage lending.

If you invest in the stock market for a long period of time, 10+ years, you can expect to earn about 7 to 10% annually on your investments.

It is worth noting, however, that this figure is *not* inflation-adjusted. This means, as I explained earlier, that inflation, the erosion of your purchasing power, is not yet considered. If you deduct the inflation rate, which typically hovers around 2% annually, from your investment return you get your *real* investment return. Inflation is important to consider, especially over long periods of time, as it decreases your purchasing power and effectively works like a tax.

Even when accounting for inflation, though, stock returns beat the returns of bonds over the long-term which tend to produce about 4 to 5% annually. Interest rates are so low since the Great Recession that I don't even want to bring regular savings accounts with their pitiful rates up as a valid investment alternative here.

Real estate also is an attractive pathway for investors to produce high annual average returns of about 10%, but this is a figure you should take with caution. There are different property types and strategies real estate investors can employ, so your mileage may vary. I will discuss ways to make passive income from real estate in Chapter 8.

Given the large amount of studies that mostly peg the long-term stock market return at approximately 7 to 8% annually, inflation-adjusted, it is reasonable to expect that investors will continue to be able to earn this kind of investment return going forward as well. The U.S. economy and the valuation of the U.S. stock market has grown consistently since the country was founded in 1776, despite multiple wars, recessions and terror attacks and chances are that the U.S. economy will keep growing.

Trading vs. Investing

Trading and investing are two totally different things, and it is paramount that you don't confuse the two. Trading and investing have nothing to do with each other, and I certainly don't stand for get-rich-quick schemes that promote day-trading, options trading, forex trading, crypto-currency trading, and other speculative endeavors that you will likely lose your shirt with.

If you want to try day-trading or other sorts of speculating, feel free to do so. It is fine as long as you understand the risks and have good market instincts. However, I don't see short-term oriented trading strategies as a basis to systematically build wealth and achieve financial freedom.

What many gurus that pitch trading strategies don't tell you is that the vast majority of people trying this stuff lose. And they lose badly. I refuse to speculate and I won't gamble away my financial future in the stock market, and neither should you. Instead, I am investing my money - using common sense, my experience, my financial background and the concepts described in this chapter - in order to construct a portfolio of high-quality dividend-paying stocks that pay me passive income while I do what I love. I sometimes refer to dividend-paying stocks as F.I.R.E. stocks because the acronym F.I.R.E. stands for Financial Independence Retire Early.

F.I.R.E. stocks are great for people that want to retire earlier than most people. All we need to do is to identify and select not more than 20 quality dividend-paying stocks that have paid shareholders a growing dividend in the past. We can easily screen for companies that meet those criteria on the internet. In fact, lots of investment sites such as www.finviz.com rank companies based on parameters you can set, e.g. market value, industry, dividend yield, or dividend growth rate.

In addition, there are plenty of websites and blogs on the internet that cover and analyze the best of the best dividend stocks. One sub-group of dividend stocks is called *Dividend Aristocrats.*

Dividend Aristocrats are companies that have raised their dividend payouts for more than 25 years in a row, which makes it highly likely that these companies will continue to raise their dividend payouts in the future. *Dividend Aristocrats* are perfect income vehicles for investors, not speculators.

I highly recommend you to start *investing* into high-quality dividend-paying stocks. Investing is a marathon and not a sprint, and it requires only a basic understanding of investments, emotional resilience, and patience. If you have that, you will do very well in the stock market, as long as you keep your emotions in check and don't gamble with your money!

Your Single Biggest Advantage: Think Long-Term!

Speculating and investing money, as I just explained, are two very different animals, and lots of people don't really seem to understand why investing and not speculating is the way to go. So let's get rid of that confusion once and for all!

When you are speculating, you are looking to make a quick profit in the stock market by buying a stock you think will increase in price. The reason for an increase in the share price could be that you expect a strong earnings release or a buyout. A speculator would buy any stock, for instance, that he or she expects to increase in price, in order to make a quick buck. Speculators buy and sell stocks fast, often without fully understanding the underlying businesses they are buying and selling. It goes without saying that this speculative strategy often depends on luck only, and it is the reason why so many people in the stock market are not consistently profitable.

Investing, on the other hand, is the polar opposite of speculating.

Investing requires investors to research and understand the companies whose stocks they buy. The investor reads investor presentations, securities filings, analyst commentary, and values companies based on metrics such as earnings, cash flow, and net assets (we will discuss valuation metrics shortly).

Investing is a serious business, for obvious reasons. For one thing, we have worked hard and delayed instant gratification for a long time in order to save up some money that we can invest. Ideally, the passive income stream that follows will allow us to retire early. As such, we owe it to ourselves to treat our savings and investment portfolio with the care of a prudent investor. The last thing you need after saving money for a year or two is to make stupid impulse decisions and gamble your financial future away in the stock market.

Today, most investors are not really investors... they merely temporarily own a few stocks, and once they make a quick buck or lose their patience, they move on to the next target. Investing, on the other hand, requires emotional resilience, primarily because the market will test your patience. It is quite common that a stock you bought drops 10, 20 or 50%. If you have done your research, however, and understand the value proposition of the stock at hand, you won't panic easily.

Assume you researched Company A and bought its stock at $100. Now, the stock market crashes and the stock drops to $70. What are you going to do?

If you panic and sell, you lose $30 per share on your investment, reflecting a whopping 30% loss. If you did your research, however, and think that nothing materially changed with respect to the prospects of your company, the price drop may constitute a buying opportunity. If you liked and bought the stock at $100 the first time, and it can now be had for $70, why not buy more? Buying more shares of a company you already own at a lower price is called *dollar cost averaging.*

The difference here is simply mindset; the speculator immediately drops the stock and realizes a loss, even though the price decline may only be temporary. The smart investor, on the other hand, buys more of Company's A stock when it is on sale.

The investor who thinks long-term and who keeps his cool during a market downturn is best positioned to come out on top. As an investor, the single biggest advantage you have in the stock market is to not take market swings too seriously and be *long-term oriented.*

This is so important that I want to repeat it again: being long-term oriented is the single biggest advantage you have in the investment game! If you are truly long-term oriented, you don't feel the need to immediately react to news and constantly trade. A long-term view in terms of investing firmly keeps your eyes on the ball - financial independence - and prevents you from making stupid, emotional decisions that can cost you a hell of a lot of money in the long run.

Risk and Return

One of the most important concepts in any undergraduate finance class at universities around the world is the relationship of risk and return, which, in theory is often explained using so called *asset pricing models.* I am going to spare you all the technical details of the various asset pricing models here because they go beyond the scope of this chapter and will only complicate things.

What you have to understand, though, is that (expected) returns tend to be positively correlated with risk: the more risky an investment is, the higher the (expected) rate of return must be in order to entice you to accept the investment risk. I have placed 'expected' returns in brackets above because in the investment world you can never be sure that you actually earn the returns that you think you will be able to earn. A simple example should provide some clarity.

I have previously alluded to the long-term annual returns of stocks falling into a broad range of 7-10%. This is an *average* only. Assume you buy stocks today and the U.S. economy drifts into a recession in the following month; stock prices will likely fall as a recession unfolds in order to reflect the bleaker economic picture (lower corporate earnings and cash flow), and investors' decreasing risk appetite. As a result, over the short haul you may earn less than 7-10%, or maybe even earn negative returns. All stock and real estate investments come with a certain amount of risk and returns are *never* guaranteed. However, if you invest for a long time, you will be able to ride out the storms in the economy and the stock market, and you can reasonably expect to earn 7-10% annually, on average.

If you happen to stumble upon an investment proposal that guarantees you a certain return, you should run as fast as you can. Guaranteed returns don't exist in the investment world!

Asset Allocation Pyramid

Generally speaking, risk and return are positively related. The more risk you take, the more money you could potentially earn. I am going to explain the relationship of risk and return using the so-called asset allocation pyramid.

At the bottom of the asset allocation pyramid you will find savings accounts and insurances that have the lowest risk and the lowest return. They are the foundation of your financial wealth because they meet your fundamental needs of safety. As you move up the hierarchy, you will find assets that have more risks, but also higher return potential.

Let's go through these asset classes one by one.

1. Savings Accounts = Lowest Risk and Lowest Return

Savings accounts with an FDIC insurance are at the bottom of the asset allocation pyramid. The Federal Deposit Insurance Corporation, or FDIC, insures bank deposits up to $250,000, if the bank is an FDIC member. Most banks in the U.S. are members of the Federal Deposit Insurance Corporation. The FDIC monitors banks and makes sure that financial institutions behave in a sound, financial manner. As a consequence, the risk associated with savings accounts is very low, which in turn means that you can also only earn a very small return on them (usually less than 1%).

2. Government Bonds = Very Safe but Low Return

U.S. government bonds are generally associated with very low risk because bonds that are issued by the U.S. government are backed by the full faith and credit of the United States. The United States has never defaulted on its debt obligations in its history which means the risk of losing your capital is very low.

U.S. government bonds are a very safe place to park your money, but the return is not that great either. Typically, you can expect to earn 1-3% annually on U.S. government bonds, depending on what maturity date you choose. Generally speaking, U.S. government bonds often barely allow you to earn the inflation rate.

3. Corporate Bonds = Higher Risk Than Government Bonds but Also Higher Returns

If you are willing to take higher investment risks, you could buy corporate bonds which, contrary to government bonds, are not backed by the resources of any government. Corporate bonds are issued by companies to finance their operations. Corporate bonds are typically categorized into different risk classes by credit agencies such as Standard & Poor's and Moody's, which assign credit ratings to the bonds so that investors can better understand the risks that are associated with such investments.

The higher a company's credit rating, the more likely it is that the company will be able to make its interest payments on time and repay the principal amount when it is due. The more likely it is that a company will make its contractual payments to bond investors, the lower the coupon rate on the bond (the interest rate) will be. If it is deemed more risky for investors to buy a corporate bond, the company issuing the bond will have to offer investors a higher coupon rate.

4. Stocks = Higher Risk Than Corporate Bonds but Also Higher Returns

If you like even more risk and potentially higher returns, you could buy stocks, which make up the next layer of the asset allocation pyramid. Companies issue stocks in order to raise capital which is then used to make new investments into the business.

Stocks can also be categorized and ranked based on risk. Companies that have been around for decades and that have strong market positions and products, brand recognition, a large customer base, and have grown earnings and cash flow over time are less risky than, say, a new disruptive start-up in Fintech, or a company that offers a new streaming service.

Stocks have very attractive return potential over the long-term, but the risk can be quite high over the short haul. Investors can use different strategies to reduce the risk associated with stocks by limiting the size of their investment positions and diversifying their portfolios.

5. Warrants = Extremely High Risk and Return Potential (As Well as Possibility of Total Loss)

Without getting into too much detail, warrants are highly speculative instruments that derive their value from an underlying asset, such as a stock, a market index, or the price of a commodity like gold. I'd recommend investors to focus on their objective of building an investment portfolio that produces durable and, preferably, growing dividend income over time, and warrants do not play a part in this.

While the potential for very high returns is extraordinarily high with warrants - you could earn hundreds of percent on your capital in a week or even in a day - you could also lose your shirt with warrants. If you seek to build long-term wealth in order to live a debt and worry-free life, my best tip is to stay away from warrants, options, and any other speculative instruments. Remember: we are investing, not speculating!

Diversification: Don't Put All Your Eggs in One Basket

Diversification is an important aspect of investing, and understanding it is a crucial component for long-term financial success. Diversifying essentially means that you are spreading your funds out over a large number of investments in order to mitigate investment risks. Not putting all of your investment eggs in one basket is key to good risk management and helps protect your net worth in case something bad happens to one of the stocks in your portfolio.

Say, for the sake of argument, that you invested 100% of your savings into just one stock: Apple. The performance of your investment portfolio now depends 100% on how Apple is doing, because it is the only stock you own. If something bad happens to Apple, for whatever reason, and the stock drops, potentially significantly, you have no way of offsetting the drop in Apple's stock price with any other investment. If, on the other hand, you put only 5% of your portfolio assets into Apple's stock, a decrease in the price of Apple's stock will now have a much lower impact on your total portfolio performance.

The key benefit to diversification is that it lowers investment risks. The more concentrated your investment portfolio is (i.e., the fewer stocks you own), the more risk is in your portfolio and the more vulnerable you are financially. On the other hand, if you are more diversified (i.e., the more stocks you own), the less risk you have in your portfolio and the better you are able to mitigate market volatility and/or deal with a recession.

One of the best ways to diversify your portfolio is to simply buy an exchange-traded fund, or ETF. Exchange-traded funds are funds that mimic the performance of an underlying index, such as the S&P 500. By buying shares of an exchange-traded fund you are essentially buying the market itself. The beauty here is that you don't have to be concerned with further diversifying your portfolio. This approach is particularly useful for investors that look for a simple, low-maintenance, time-and-cost-efficient investment strategy and don't want to be too involved in the investment game.

However, if you choose to actively manage your portfolio yourself, you should definitely attempt to diversify your portfolio, for the exact reasons I just mentioned.

Ideally, when you construct your own investment portfolio, you would want to spread your funds out over a number of different companies with different sizes in different industries. Thus, you will be less exposed to a downturn that affects only a certain industry or a certain geography.

Your portfolio should also include assets of different asset classes (REITs, stocks, bonds, commodities), and you might want to consider foreign stocks as well in order to become less exposed to the economy in your home country. Investing something like 5-10% internationally (either in the form of stocks, bonds, or exchange-traded funds) is a great way of including promising international companies and markets in your portfolio. A good example for a U.S. investor would be to consider emerging market stocks, e.g. from China, which tend to grow very fast due to the overall rise of China as an economic power. A good example for a non-U.S. investor would be to consider an investment in Facebook, for example, which is the world's largest social media company and which has the most efficient advertising platform in the world.

In addition, you might want to limit the size of any individual portfolio position. I generally make sure that my *highest* conviction ideas don't account for more than 10% of my total portfolio value. For instance, I believe that Realty Income's stock will be a top stock to own for the next couple of decades. If my portfolio is valued at $100,000 today, then I would still want to make sure that I am not investing more than $10,000 ($100,000 x 0.1) into Realty Income at this point. Realty Income may be a good stock for income investors (and I will discuss why in the case study that follows in the next chapter), but that doesn't mean that the real estate industry could not consolidate considerably during the next recession. Even top stocks occasionally fall out-of-favor and drop in price.

While I cap my top ideas at 10% of my total portfolio value, good investment ideas generally don't exceed the 5% threshold. Limiting the size of your portfolio positions effectively allows you to control risk and hedge your portfolio in such a way that an individual stock position does not have an extraordinarily large influence on your total portfolio performance.

I generally aim to have a good mix of between 20 and 30 high-quality stocks in my income portfolio, but you don't need to have this many, especially not if you follow a passive investing approach (exchange-traded funds). Studies have shown that owning from 12 to 18 stocks in your investment portfolio will allow you to reap ~90% of the benefits of diversification. You reach full diversification when you simply hold the market portfolio through an exchange-traded fund, for example.

The value of a diversified stock portfolio reveals itself during times of heightened market volatility, poor investor sentiment, and an overall decline in investors' willingness to accept risk. This is usually the case when investors start to expect either a recession, or weaker corporate earnings. Investors generally avoid investing in risk assets like stocks during such times and rather invest in so-called safe haven assets like gold, or the U.S. Dollar.

Telecommunication, utility, and health care stocks tend to do better than the average stock during a recession as well. The reason is that despite weak economic activity, people still demand internet services, electricity, and health care, and demand for such products tends to be relatively stable.

Assume, for instance, that the U.S. economy is about to fall into a recession. A diversified portfolio that includes stocks of health care and utility companies with fairly stable earnings is likely going to perform much better than a portfolio consisting entirely of technology stocks. Diversification cushions the blow and limits downside risks, which is exactly what we are looking for. Remember, protecting the capital we worked so hard to build in the first place is our primary goal.

ETFs and Mutual Funds

You can choose into which asset classes you invest your money (cash, stocks, bonds, stocks, real estate etc.), and you can also choose whether you manage your portfolio *actively* or *passively*.

In an active management approach you manage your money yourself. This means you make your own investment decisions, research the stocks you want to buy, review your investment portfolio regularly, and periodically rebalance your portfolio in order to account for changes in your own personal situation, or in the mix of assets you want to own going forward. Alternatively, you could decide to outsource these responsibilities to a fund manager who specializes in managing investors' money. Most often, investors delegate active fund management responsibilities to mutual fund managers.

Mutual funds are investment pools managed by professional money managers who will charge you a hefty fee for the privilege of investing your money. Almost all major investment companies offer mutual fund products today that have specific investment mandates, such as investing only in growth stocks, or only in bonds, or only in stocks of a certain country or geography. Mutual funds do not try to mimic the performance of a major stock market index, but instead seek to pick stocks that the active manager thinks are undervalued and have potential to outperform the broader market.

On the other end of the spectrum are passive investment approaches which have gained in popularity over the last couple of years as investors started to put more money into so-called exchange-traded funds. The goal of an ETF is to track the return of an underlying price index, most often a stock index.

An exchange-traded fund can be bought and sold just like any other stock on the stock exchange through your broker. For example, you could buy an exchange-traded fund that mimics the performance of the S&P 500 index such as Vanguard's S&P 500 ETF, which can be bought on the stock exchange and has the ticker symbol VOO. When you buy an ETF that tracks the S&P 500, you are essentially buying the S&P 500 itself: If the S&P 500 stock index gains 1% in any given day, the shares of the ETF can also be expected to rise about 1% in price. You can buy ETFs either through a broker such as TD Ameritrade, E-Trade, and Interactive Brokers, or directly through large fund management companies such as Fidelity or Vanguard.

Since exchange-traded funds simply invest in companies that make up a stock index, they don't require expensive analysts to conduct extensive stock analysis. As a consequence, exchange-traded funds have a much more efficient cost structure than mutual funds. ETFs are very cost efficient and often have expense ratios well below 1% whereas mutual funds tend to be much more costly; expense ratios of 3% or more are not at all uncommon in the mutual fund world. Vanguard's S&P 500 ETF, on the other hand, has an expense ratio of only 0.03 percent. An expensive mutual fund can cost you tens of thousands of dollars over long periods of time, which is a steep price to pay for a manager that is unlikely to beat the market return.

There is a heated debate in the investor community going on about the use of ETFs, or so-called indexing strategies. This is partly because Warren Buffett himself recommended investors to build long-term wealth by investing in low-cost index funds.

Why the debate?

Because performance studies have shown over and over again that the overwhelming number of active managers in the mutual funds industry (90% or more) simply can't beat the market performance over longer periods of time. Outperforming a market index, such as the S&P 500, through a selection of hand-picked stocks is a very hard thing to do, and most fund managers fail at it. And that's a big problem for investors because if professional portfolio managers can't produce the return that the stock market index produces, what justification is there for people to invest in their funds? As a matter of fact, the performance record of many portfolio managers looks even worse when fees are considered, which are a lot higher for mutual funds than they are for exchange-traded funds.

Your best option, if you want to build wealth long-term and don't want to manage your own portfolio or devote time and energy to investing, is to simply invest your money into an exchange-traded fund, and **not** into a mutual fund.

Study after study has shown that the fees you pay for your (underperforming) mutual fund manager alone will amount to a small fortune over time. Plus, the odds are tilted against the mutual fund manager in the long-term as most fail to beat the market. Your best option, therefore, if you want to build long-term wealth but don't care so much about producing recurring monthly dividend income from your F.I.R.E. stocks, is to simply invest your money into a large exchange-traded fund, such as the Vanguard ETF mentioned above. What you should do, in fact, is make regular contributions to your exchange-traded fund, independent of the state of the capital markets or the newspaper headlines you read on a daily basis.

Target Date Funds

Target date funds are typically mutual funds that provide investment solutions to individuals that don't want to get involved too much in investing. I have already discussed my reservations with respect to active managers because they generally perform poorly and their fees really hurt your investment returns over the long haul.

Nonetheless, target date funds fulfill an important function for investors that look for a one-stop solution to their retirement planning needs.

A target date fund considers that you need your capital on a certain date, hence the name *target date fund*. The target date is typically the year you plan to retire. If you plan to retire in 2050, for example, you would choose a target date fund with a 2050 target date.

Target date funds invest your money into more aggressive growth stocks in earlier years and gradually shift funds into safer assets, typically bonds, as you get older and reach your retirement age. As you approach your retirement age, a target date fund will consider your diminished ability to deal with risk, and will prioritize safety by investing in investment-grade rated bonds and government bonds. As long as investors are young, they can afford to take bigger risks as they have more time on their side to ride out market downturns. When investors get older, their ability to deal with risk decreases considerably..

The main benefit of a target date fund is that it provides a simple, one-stop solution to your retirement needs and that it considers that you will retire in a pre-determined year. The target date fund will also change its asset allocation over time and turn more conservative as the target date approaches. On the flip side, target date funds are typically actively managed which means that expenses will be higher than with a pure passive indexing strategy (buying an ETF). Also, like all actively managed funds, target date funds do have investment and underperformance risks.

If you have an interest in investing and need to produce passive income, I would recommend you to build a portfolio of F.I.R.E. stocks yourself.

Of course, this approach requires you to do some work. It requires that you regularly follow the financial news, at least to some degree. Tune in to Bloomberg or CNBC every once in a while and skip through an investor presentation of a company whose products you like. I have mentioned F.I.R.E. stocks a couple of times so far, but not yet explained what kind of criteria they need to meet. And that is what we are going to discuss next.

Key Takeaways

● Generate your own investment ideas and learn from the best investors in the field. A good starting point is to invest in companies whose products you personally like;

● Over the long-term, stocks have produced annual returns of approximately 10%, on average. Inflation-adjusted, you can probably expect to earn 7-8% annually, on average;

● There is a profound difference between short-term focused speculators and long-term minded investors. Your single biggest advantage in the stock market is to play the long game and remain unimpressed by market swings;

● The best strategy for most investors is to simply invest in a low-cost exchange-traded fund that tracks the performance of a major stock market index such as the S&P 500;

● Mutual funds are a scam because they are expensive and because most mutual fund managers can't outperform the stock market;

● Target date funds are vehicles that adjust their asset allocations as the target/retirement date approaches;

● If you are buying F.I.R.E. stocks to produce passive income for you, diversification is crucial to limit downside risks.

CHAPTER 7

PASSIVE INCOME THROUGH
DIVIDEND INVESTING

"If you don't find a way to make money while you sleep,

you will work until you die."

- Warren Buffett

The overarching goal for aspiring early retirees should be to build a portfolio of F.I.R.E. stocks that have a reasonable chance of growing their dividend payouts over a long period of time, so that we can live off of the passive income those stocks produce. But, there are thousands of stocks available in the U.S. stock market alone that are worth trillions of dollars. How do you know which stock is a good one to buy?

One way to find a good stock to buy for your dividend portfolio is to simply look for stocks of companies that have done well in the past. That's right. There are a lot of stocks in the stock market, but not that many actually have produced stable returns and grown their dividend payouts over time. And that's exactly what we are looking for; we are looking for resilient companies that can grow their dividends even when the U.S. economy is in a recession and times are tougher than usual.

One group of stocks that has achieved that and that is worth keeping a close eye on are so-called *Dividend Aristocrats* which I briefly mentioned in the last chapter. If you remember, *Dividend Aristocrats* are stocks of companies that have grown their dividends for at least 25 years in a row, independent of the prevailing economic climate. Companies that have raised their dividends for 25 consecutive years are mainly large, well-known corporations, including telecommunications company AT&T, oil and gas driller Exxon Mobil Corp., fast food chain McDonald's, and beverage company Coca-Cola. Currently, 57 stocks are included in the Standard & Poor's Dividend Aristocrat index and the group of elite stocks is growing as more companies meet the hurdle of growing their payouts for 25+ years.

Now, even though *Dividend Aristocrats* have raised their payouts like clockwork over the last quarter century, there is no guarantee that these companies will continue to raise their payouts in the future. Bad things happen all the time: companies run into financial trouble, go bankrupt, are forced to restructure, are out-competed by disruptive newcomers, or are taken over. While there are no hard guarantees that *Dividend Aristocrats* will continue to grow their dividends going forward, the odds are nonetheless strongly titled in favor of this happening. A company that has done well over the last 25 years and that has been shareholder-friendly will probably do just as well in the future.

Screening for *Dividend Aristocrats* is a great way of finding companies with shareholder-friendly management and proven records of consistent value creation.

Besides a growing dividend, however, there are other factors that F.I.R.E. investors may want to consider. Personally, I follow a rigid checklist before I buy a stock for my income portfolio, in order to systematize the investment process and reduce the probability of making mistakes. Here are a couple of things I look for in a F.I.R.E. company and stock:

● Management has proven to be competent and shareholder-friendly;

● Management has a proven record of execution (management follows through with what it says);

● The company does business ethically, meaning it has not been fined for misdeeds and violations of best practices;

● The company preferably has a diversified business model, meaning it does not depend on only one revenue stream to fund its dividend to shareholders;

● It has a conservative balance sheet, which limits downside risks for investors and adds a layer of security in case times get tough;

● The company has a history of earnings and cash flow growth;

● The company has paid a dividend consistently over time, and grown its payout independent of the state of the U.S. economy;

- The company pays either a monthly or quarterly dividend;

- The dividend has grown consistently at a 2-3% annual growth rate in order to offset the negative effect of inflation;

- Shares aren't overvalued based on historical standards or relative to peers.

This list is a pretty good starting point for further stock analysis because it narrows down the number of potential stocks to buy for your F.I.R.E. portfolio considerably. You can use this checklist to guide your investment decisions and screen for high-quality dividend-paying stocks.

REITs as Income Vehicles

A REIT, or real estate investment trust, is a special kind of real estate investment company. The shares of a REIT trade on the stock exchange just like stocks of all the other publicly-listed companies. REITs are an important group of F.I.R.E. stocks to discuss because of their unique qualification for creating passive income.

A lot of stocks, though not all of them, pay shareholders a regular dividend in order to let them participate in the success of the business. A company that does well financially may decide to pay out a certain percentage of its profits as dividends to shareholders. The portion of a company's profits that is not paid out as dividends is retained and can be used for other purposes, such as making growth investments, or building a capital cushion.

A lot of companies decide to pay out 40% or 50% of their profits to their shareholders in order to strike a balance between rewarding shareholders on one hand and reinvesting into their businesses on the other hand.

Real estate investment trusts are corporations that tend to have very high payout ratios (70% or higher). Real estate investment trusts are tax-advantaged income vehicles and the Internal Revenue Service in the U.S. requires REITs to distribute at least 90% of their taxable income to the shareholders of the company. A real estate investment trust does not pay tax on the corporate level, but the shareholders of the REIT are subject to taxation.

The tax-advantaged corporate structure means that REITs are perfect income vehicles for investors that seek to create passive income, and the majority of my personal income is derived from investments in a small group of such REITs. Due to the payout requirement (distribution of 90% of profits), REITs tend to have very attractive dividend yields ranging from 3-5% for very fast-growing REITs to 7-12% for more risky and leveraged real estate finance companies and mortgage REITs.

Most REITs pay their dividends quarterly, meaning investors get four dividends annually, paid every three months. Some REITs, such as Realty Income, pay a monthly dividend which can give investors more income security. Some REITs may also decide to pay a special one-time cash dividend, for instance when the trust had a particularly strong financial year or is drowning in cash because it sold some assets.

Ideally, though, our REIT stocks should pay a predictable dividend every quarter or every month. The reason is that special dividends are nice, but there is a huge drawback to them: we can't plan for them and we can't hope to receive special dividends in order to cover our living expenses. We need predictable income from our investment portfolio in order to make sure that we can pay our bills.

REITs, in my estimation, provide a great pathway for aspiring early retirees to build both long-term wealth and create passive income. With that being said, let's jump into a REIT case study in order to see what a desirable F.I.R.E. stock really looks like.

Case Study: Realty Income Corp.

[Full disclosure: I own shares of Realty Income in my own dividend growth portfolio. I am not compensated by or affiliated with Realty Income in any way, however I believe that this REIT makes an illustrative example for what to look for in a F.I.R.E. stock]

Realty Income is a commercial property real estate investment trust in the United States with a market capitalization of more than $22 billion. Realty Income is a so-called net-lease REIT, meaning the company's tenants are responsible for property-related expenses such as maintenance, taxes, insurance and repair costs, which are typically items the landlord is responsible for.

Realty Income's retail properties are leased to the company's tenants based on long-term rental agreements that provide the company and its shareholders with long-term cash flow stability. Realty Income acquires new properties regularly and leases the properties to large retail companies, pharmacy chains, fitness clubs, dollar stores, logistics companies, and so on. The five largest tenants for Realty Income, for instance, are Walgreens, 7-Eleven, Fed-Ex, Dollar General and LA Fitness.

Realty Income's tenants make contractual lease payments to the REIT every month. Realty Income deducts its operating expenses from its rental revenues and then pays out a large share of its income to the shareholders of the business as dividends. Realty Income pays its dividend monthly and the real estate investment trust has consistently grown its payout since the company was listed on the New York Stock Exchange in 1994.

Realty Income, in fact, checks all of the boxes of a high-quality dividend stock:

● Management has been really good on execution: The REIT has regularly acquired new properties and integrated them into its real estate platform. Buying new properties at reasonable prices is a great way of producing additional earnings and cash flow, which in turn boded well for a higher monthly dividend over time;

● Management is extremely shareholder-friendly: The real estate company hikes its monthly dividend regularly by small amounts, which compound greatly over time;

● Management is conservative in its business approach: The REIT has a conservative balance sheet with investment-grade credit ratings that help protect the company in case the U.S. real estate market or the U.S. economy crash again;

● Realty Income's occupancy rate - a key indicator of portfolio and business quality - has never fallen below 96% since 1994. Despite multiple economic booms and busts in the last 25 years, Realty Income has been able to almost fully rent out its properties which ensured stable rental income. This is another key feature we are looking for in a F.I.R.E. stock: we want to be sure that a company can earn money and pay a dividend even when times are tough;

● Management prioritizes diversification: The company has a large, geographically diversified real estate portfolio, meaning Realty Income's commercial properties can be found in 49 states and Puerto Rico, and the company has most recently entered the U.K. market through a transaction with retail company Sainsbury's. The more diversified a REIT is, the safer the REIT's cash flows are. Assume that one of Realty Income's tenants runs into trouble and can't make lease payments. Since Realty Income has small exposure to each individual tenant, the REIT's cash flows are only impacted marginally, which in turn means the company will continue to be able to make dividend payments;

● Realty Income has a highly credible earnings history. The REIT has grown its earnings in 22 out of 23 years (performance period 1996-2018) and achieved average annual earnings growth of 5.1%. Only in 2009, at the height of the real estate crisis, did Realty Income post negative earnings growth of a moderate 2.1%;

- Realty Income is a recession-proof income vehicle because the company has paid a growing dividend since 1994, no matter how the stock market or the economy did. Realty Income has raised its dividend payout even throughout the Great Recession in 2008/9 which was a terrible time for real estate companies;

- Realty Income's ability to grow earnings has led to an incredible dividend growth history. Since the company went public on the New York Stock Exchange in 1994, Realty Income has grown its annual dividend from $0.90/share to $2.71/share in 2018, reflecting 201.1% dividend growth, or 4.7% compound annual dividend growth. The company also handed shareholders 101 dividend increases since 1994 (as of the first quarter of 2019), and pays shareholders on a monthly basis;

- If you purchased 1,000 shares of Realty Income on December 31, 2008, you would have paid $23,150. If you held those shares until June 30, 2019, your investment value would have risen to $68,970. At the time of purchase, you would have collected $1,701 annually in dividends. Thanks to Realty Income's excellent dividend growth history, investors that stuck with the REIT for more than a decade now collect $2,718 annually in dividends, reflecting an increase of approximately 60% in dividend income;

- A high-quality income vehicle like Realty Income that is extremely transparent and shareholder-friendly and that offers investors a high degree of dividend safety, obviously, is not cheap. The REIT's share price has steadily appreciated over time as investors caught on to Realty Income's strong value proposition. Thus, Realty Income's shares sell for a premium multiple: 20x. This means that income investors pay 20 times this year's estimated funds from operations for the REIT (the terms *funds from operations* is a cash flow term that is used to value real estate investment trusts). Quality always has its price;

● Realty Income's current dividend yield is 3.6 percent.

I have used this case study in order to highlight what characteristics I look for in a F.I.R.E. stock that I want to buy for my own income portfolio. I love REITs like Realty Income because of the reliability of their passive income, implied growth potential and little maintenance requirement. Obviously, I own a lot of other stocks too, both inside and outside the REIT sector. Real estate investment trusts, however, are excellent income vehicles for aspiring early retirees because of the ease with which they produce dividend income. Once you buy a F.I.R.E. stock like Realty Income, all you need to do is lean back, relax, and collect your dividend checks. Time and compounding will do most of the heavy lifting for you. The hard times of saving, budgeting, and investing money are now slowly starting to pay off.

F.I.R.E. Stocks That Produce Passive Dividend Income

The beauty of a diversified stock portfolio consisting of high-quality dividend-paying stocks is that market ups and downs won't matter all that much. As long as we have exercised good due diligence and bought solid F.I.R.E. stocks at good prices, market volatility should not concern us in the least. We can just sit back, relax and let time do the work for us. As we will see in Chapter 9, the simple practice of reinvesting your investment returns (dividends, interest, rental income) will turbocharge your ability to retire early.

Every passive income-oriented stock portfolio should include a large number of high-quality REITs and *Dividend Aristocrats* that have the potential to produce attractive dividend income over time. Besides Realty Income, which is often referred to as the gold standard in the income investor community, other potentially attractive F.I.R.E. stocks include:

Commercial Property REITs (Low-to-Moderate risk)

- Realty Income (O)
- National Retail Properties (NNN)
- STORE Capital (STOR)
- W.P. Carey (WPC)
- Lexington Realty Trust (LXP)
- STAG Industrial (STAG)

Health Care REITs (Low-to-Moderate risk)

- Ventas (VTR)
- HCP (HCP)
- Welltower (WELL)

- LTC Properties (LTC)

- Physicians Realty Trust (DOC)

- Medical Properties Trust (MPW)

- National Health Investors (NHI)

Data Center REITs (Medium risk)

- Digital Realty Trust (DLR)

- CoreSite Realty (COR)

Dividend Aristocrats (Medium risk)

- AbbVie (ABBV)

- Abbott Laboratories (ABT)

- Archer-Daniels-Midland (ADM)

- AT&T (T)

- Chevron (CVX)

- Coca-Cola Company (KO)

- Colgate-Palmolive (CL)

- Emerson Electric (EMR)

- Exxon Mobil (XOM)

- Federal Realty Investment Trust (FRT)

- Johnson & Johnson (JNJ)

- Kimberly-Clark (KMB)

- Lowe's Companies (LOW)

- McDonald's (MCD)

- PepsiCo (PEP)

- Target (TGT)

- Walmart (WMT)

- Walgreens Boots Alliance (WBA)

Business Development Companies (High risk)

- Main Street Capital (MAIN)

- Goldman Sachs BDC (GSBD)

- Hercules Capital (HTGC)

- TPG Specialty Lending (TSLX)

- Gladstone Investment (GAIN)

If you don't know what stocks to buy, consider any of the low-to-medium risk companies listed above. A total of 57 S&P 500 stocks are classified as *Dividend Aristocrats*, so the list provided here is not complete. Many of the companies mentioned here have managed to grow their businesses for decades and are often leaders in their respective industries.

Oil companies such as Exxon Mobil Corp., for example, should do well during an economic upswing when energy prices increase, while telecommunications firms such as AT&T can be expected to do reasonably well even when the economy is in a recession, and the same is true for companies that produce toothpaste, breakfast cereals, or tissue paper.

As a matter of fact, REITs and business development companies make up the majority of stocks in my own income portfolio. Business development companies, or BDCs, are lending companies that make loans to other businesses and collect interest in return. These companies are also tax-advantaged and their stocks often produce dividend yields of 7% or higher. That being said, business development companies also have higher risks than low-yielding real estate investment trusts.

Of course, the list provided above is merely a starting point and should not replace your own due diligence. You must also take into consideration what kind of risk you are willing to take and for how long you want to invest. Again, if you have any questions about specific stocks, don't hesitate to shoot me an email: chris@retiredby35.com.

Doubling Down on F.I.R.E. Stocks

We don't just want to buy dividend-paying stocks once and then never look at them again. What we really want to do is take advantage of circumstances when our F.I.R.E. stocks drop in price and go on sale. Generally speaking, I am a buy-and-hold investor, meaning I do my research first, buy a stock if I like what I see, and then preferably hold on to the stock for the next 5, 10, or 20 years.

What I also regularly do is double down on stocks when they are out-of-favor if they have produced good returns in the past. There are two major ways you, too, can and should double down on F.I.R.E. stocks and increase the long-term earnings and dividend power of your portfolio in order to achieve financial independence:

1. DRIP

DRIP stands for dividend reinvestment plan (DRIP) and is a program that allows shareholders of the company to invest their dividends into additional shares of the company instead of receiving a cash dividend. Realty Income and many other companies have formal dividend reinvestment plans where you can sign up and receive additional shares instead of cash.

For instance, say you own 1,000 shares of Company A that pay you $120/year in dividends. When you sign up for a dividend reinvestment plan, or DRIP, you can choose to receive the $120 worth of dividends in additional shares. If Company A's shares sell for $10 each, for example, you would get 12 additional shares.

Utilizing a dividend reinvestment plan is a form of dollar cost averaging. In a nutshell, dollar cost averaging means you are buying stock A periodically for a set amount of dollars each time. The idea is that you are smoothing out the effects of market volatility and lower your cost base over time.

Here's an example of how dollar cost averaging works in practice. Assume you choose to invest $1,000/month into a quality stock such as Realty Income. In this plan, you are purchasing $1,000 worth of shares on the 1ˢᵗ day of each month. If the share price for Realty Income is $50 on January 1, 20xx, you can buy 20 shares. If the share price drops to $45 by February 1, 20xx, then your $1,000 are now buying 22 shares. If the stock price drops further to $40 on March 1, 20xx, you can buy 25 shares. Let's say the stock goes sideways and you continue to add about 25 shares each month for the rest of the year. After one year, how does the math look like?

You bought a total of 292 shares (Jan: 20, Feb: 22, Mar-Dec: 25/month) for $12,000 ($1,000/month x 12). The average cost of your position after one year is $41.10/share ($12,000 / 292 shares) which means you were able to reduce the *average cost* of your position from $50 in January 20xx to $41 throughout the year, because you continuously bought the stock at a price below $50. If Realty Income's stock now happens to rebound, or the economy starts to pick up steam again and asset prices recover, the lowered cost basis will work in your favor and allow you to reap higher returns.

A 401(k) plan, for instance, effectively uses dollar cost averaging. The employee sets a pre-determined amount of his or her paycheck to buy stocks, bonds, funds or a combination of them. Independent of how the market is doing or how low or high interest rates are, a 401(k) invests the same dollar amount (assuming you don't change your contribution or see an increase/decrease in your salary) into the same mix of assets that you have selected.

Dollar cost averaging can be a highly effective strategy, and I highly recommend it, especially when you purchase an exchange-traded fund or high-quality dividend-paying stocks on a regular basis.

2. Buy Stocks When They are Out-Of-Favor

Another great way of reaching financial independence a little bit faster and turbocharging your passive income potential is by doubling down on stocks during a recession. During an economic downturn, investors don't like to invest in stocks due to larger risks to a company's revenues, earnings, and cash flow. In addition, bankruptcy risks rise during a recession, which is why stocks are typically widely underpriced during an economic downturn. Obviously, smart income investors with a long-term investment horizon and some cash saved up are at an advantage here.

The single best thing you can do as an investor, generally speaking, is to buy F.I.R.E. stocks when nobody wants them, because that's when they are really cheap. Buying blue-chip stocks - stocks of well-known companies that signify quality and reliability - when they are out-of-favor is an excellent way to start building long-term wealth and creating a stream of passive income for decades to come.

One key component of long-term financial success is to not let daily news stories distract you from your long-term financial goals. One stock market adage that has been widely popularized by Warren Buffett is this one:

"Be fearful when others are greedy, and be greedy when others are fearful."

In a nutshell, it means you should be very careful with investing in the stock market when investors are euphorically buying stocks (which happens at or near market tops). On the other hand, when investors are overly pessimistic about the outlook for the economy and shun stocks (which happens during market troughs), this is the best time to buy stocks.

The biggest obstacle to executing this strategy - buying stocks at a time when uncertainty and fear prevail in the stock market - will be to overcome your own emotions. When economies slide into recessions, investors tend to be scared and fearful, and, like I said, tend to stay away from stocks altogether due to their higher perceived risk during a downturn. Most people have real troubles going against the flow and doing the opposite of what most investors do in the market. If you take the long view and focus only on purchasing high-quality dividend-paying stocks or exchange-traded funds, however, this strategy can yield tremendous results in the long-term.

How to Value a Stock

When you are beginning to build a stock portfolio, the question that ultimately arises is, how much should you pay for an individual stock? A stock simply is a piece of a business that trades on a stock exchange, and its price fluctuates constantly based on a lot of different factors. Often stock prices move without a clear indication for why they are moving.

How do you determine, then, whether a stock that trades at, say, $20, is attractively priced? Is the stock overvalued, undervalued, or fairly valued at $20?

Ideally, we would want to buy stocks that are *undervalued*, meaning we want to buy a F.I.R.E. stock for a lower price than we think it is really worth. If we determine, for instance, that a F.I.R.E. stock is really worth $30, then paying just $20 would be a really good deal for us, obviously. If the stock is overvalued, however, meaning its market price exceeds our fair value estimate, we would want to pass on the purchase and look elsewhere for more attractively priced stocks to buy.

The most straightforward way to get a feeling about whether a stock is overvalued, undervalued, or fairly valued is to see what price targets analysts put on stocks. This is not a perfect approach, though, because analysts often get things wrong, too. As such, you should not entirely rely on analysts' fair value estimates or price targets. At the time of writing, for example, Apple's stock price is $180 while analysts have a consensus price target on Apple's stock of $205, indicating approximately 14% upside potential. The majority of analysts also currently believe that Apple's stock is a "Buy." You can easily check how many analysts recommend a stock and what their corresponding price targets are by going to websites like www.cnbc.com, www.nasdaq.com, or www.yahoofinance.com, which consolidate all that information.

Analysts' price targets are never perfect and are an indicative value only, but they nonetheless make for a good starting point when it comes to analyzing stocks. Most analysts value stocks based on so called price-to-earnings ratios, meaning they apply a multiple to a company's estimated earnings in order to determine its fair value. A simple example will illustrate this.

Assume the market estimates that Apple will earn $14/share in profits next year. Applying an earnings multiple of 15x (which is very reasonable for a fast-growing tech company) computes to a fair value estimate of $210 ($14/share x 15 earnings multiple). Since Apple's stock currently sells for just $180, the stock appears to be undervalued. There is not much more to it, really.

Valuing stocks based on expected earnings is industry standard and a very straightforward approach. There are other ratios, such as the price-to-sales ratio, which is often used to value companies that are not yet profitable, and the price-to-book-value ratio, which is often used to value banks and insurance companies with a significant amount of liquid assets on their balance sheets. The beauty is that you don't have to calculate these ratios yourself; most financial websites calculate them for you.

As a rule of thumb, stocks that have an earnings multiple below 10x are considered cheap, while companies with an earnings multiple between 10 and 15x are considered moderately valued. Companies with earnings multiples exceeding 15x can be considered highly valued, unless we are dealing with extremely fast-growing, disruptive companies that have the potential to become dominant players in their respective industries.

Again, these are only general guidelines, though, but I would say that they hold mostly true as long as we are evaluating large companies with an established market position, mature revenues and earnings, and a demonstrated history of earnings and dividend growth.

Of course, occasionally you can find a stock that sells for less than 10x earnings, but there may be a very good reason for why the stock is so cheap. Many times, very low earnings multiples point to problems; companies with low earnings multiples may be highly unprofitable, or face industry headwinds, or have debt issues.

Retail and auto companies make for good examples of companies whose stocks often have low earnings multiples. The retail industry is an industry of fierce price competition and it has low barriers to entry, which is putting huge pressure on margins. Large e-Commerce businesses such as Amazon.com with aggressive price strategies dominate the market (and have very high earnings multiples), which is why brick-and-mortar stores continue to struggle. Large traditional department store chains such as JC Penney or Sears are reducing their store footprints and closing underperforming stores because of margin pressure. Obviously, investors are not prepared to pay top dollar and top earnings multiples for struggling retail companies with negative revenue trends and persistent net losses.

The same is true for U.S. auto companies. General Motors and Ford Motor face fierce competition from electric car manufacturers, and the business is highly cyclical. Further, U.S. auto companies have struggled historically at being consistently profitable. Why would any serious investor pay a high earnings multiple for a U.S. auto company when chances are that the next industry downturn will lead to renewed margin and restructuring pressures?

REIT stocks are typically valued on a price-to-FFO basis. FFO stands for *funds from operations* and is a cash flow figure that investors use to value real estate investment trusts. Earnings are different from cash flow because a company's earnings typically include non-cash items such as depreciation. Depreciation is purely an accounting entry, not a real "cash expense". As such, REIT investors use the funds from operations figure for purposes of valuation in order to adjust for the presence of non-cash items. This adjustment gives investors a more accurate picture of a REIT's true earnings power.

Realty Income's shares, for example, currently sell for 20x this year's expected funds from operations, and the REIT has often sold for such a high FFO-multiple in the past. This implies that the current 20x FFO multiple is *not* driven by a current phase of market exuberance, but rather by investors' willingness to appreciate Realty Income's earnings and dividend reliability.

If Realty Income's FFO-multiple, for whatever reason, drops from 20x to, say, 16x, this might be a good opportunity for income investors to buy the stock. Occasionally, good stocks sell off, too, for instance during an industry downturn, or when a U.S. recession starts to unravel. Such events can cause investors to value safety (cash, gold, and bonds) more than risk assets (stocks). The smart investor seeking early retirement would want to take advantage of such temporary periods of market distress and purchase high-quality F.I.R.E. stocks whenever they are out-of-favor.

The previously highlighted checklist of what to look for in high-quality dividend-paying stocks should make sure that you buy only stocks that meet our investment criteria and that have a high chance of growing their dividend payouts slowly but steadily over time.

Millennial Investors

If you are a millennial investor, following the advice in this book as it relates to saving, budgeting, and investing will make a profound difference in your life, long term, as long as you stick to the principles discussed here.

Millennial investors, in particular, have one advantage over other investors: they are young, and therefore have **time**. And time works like magic for your investment portfolio. If you are 20 or 25 and the economy falls into a recession, you have plenty of time to ride out the downturn and make additional investments in the stock market. On the other hand, if you are 60 and depend on your portfolio for income, and the economy slides into a recession, you are facing major problems. Target date funds, as previously discussed, can solve this problem by gradually shifting more funds into more conservative assets as the target date approaches.

Millennial investors can afford to take more risk than the average investor in the stock market, which means millennials can invest more money into growth stocks. Growth stocks are stocks of companies that experience massive growth due to their disruptive business models and therefore don't tend to pay a dividend. Companies whose stocks can be classified as growth stocks are Facebook, Apple, Amazon, Netflix, Google, Pinterest, Uber, Airbnb, and Tesla.

What all of these companies have in common is that they are growing extremely fast and often challenge the status quo in their respective industries. Growth companies tend to reinvest every dollar they make into their businesses to support their growth, which means they typically don't reward shareholders with a dividend. That being said, though, the value of such stocks and the value of your investment portfolio can increase significantly over time, if you get in early.

Value stocks, on the other hand, are Coca-Cola, Procter & Gamble, ExxonMobil, Chevron, and Realty Income. These are typically mature companies with large product portfolios and billions of dollars in revenues. Mature companies have very predictable cash flows and these companies tend to distribute a large chunk of their earnings to shareholders as dividends.

If you want to retire early and collect passive income, you obviously must invest in income-producing stocks that pay you an attractive dividend. For the most part, companies that fit this bill are established blue-chip companies with a demonstrated history of earnings and dividend growth throughout the business cycle. The list of REITs and *Dividend Aristocrats* provided here makes for a good starting point to kick off your investment journey.

10 Beginner Mistakes to Avoid

I have made every mistake in the book when it comes to investing, and chances are you are going to make at least some mistakes, too. And that's ok. That being said, though, the smart thing for you to do would be to learn from *my* mistakes, which will save you a lot of money, time, and nerves in the long run.

In order to navigate the tricky waters of the stock market successfully, novice investors should try to keep these 10 things in mind:

1. Know What You Are Doing

This one sounds quite intuitive, but believe me, it isn't. Too often investors rush to buy stocks when an analyst issues a "Buy" recommendation for a specific stock, hoping to make a quick buck. It is important that you know a thing or two about your future stock investments, so spend some time reading up on the company you are interested in. Always do your own research and don't buy a stock just because someone else, an analyst, or your uncle recommended it.

2. Only Invest Money That You Can Afford to Lose

There is nothing worse in life than losing money you can't afford to lose on a soured stock investment! Only invest money that you can afford to lose (worst case scenario) and that you don't depend on in order to make ends meet. Never ever speculate with your emergency fund or the down payment for your house.

3. Diversify

Don't put all your eggs in one basket. If you put 100% of your funds into stock A and the company messes up, gets sued by a competitor, faces unfavorable regulation, or goes out of business, you are in *big* trouble. Spread your risk and invest in different companies that preferably operate in different industries. Alternatively, simply buy a large, low-cost ETF that tracks a major stock market index.

4. Don't Speculate

The majority of stock investors out there are not really investors, but speculators. They hope to make a quick buck on stock price movements which by definition is speculative. Investing, on the other hand, requires you to do your homework and look into the companies that you are investing in.

5. Keep Your Emotions in Check

This is a big one. Allowing your emotions to control you is probably the single biggest reason why most investors are not successful in the stock market over the long haul. Our emotions play tricks on us all the time, and that's especially true if we have money on the line and the stock market goes on a roller coaster ride.

I *highly* recommend you to read Benjamin Graham's book *The Intelligent Investor*, especially chapters eight and twenty, which discuss how investors should handle market volatility and deal with their emotions. Warren Buffett highly recommends these chapters for both professional and novice investors. Reading this book with an open mind can save you a lot of money in the long run. It is a very insightful read indeed.

6. Don't Panic

Never, ever panic when it comes to your stock investments. The stock market sometimes makes crazy swings which can put investors' nerves to the test. The cardinal rule here is to never make a decision when you feel panic overtaking you. Doing nothing is often the best investment strategy.

7. Pick Quality Dividend-Paying Stocks

There are lots of different investment strategies investors can choose from: growth investing, value investing, high-yield investing, etc. Everyone can find a strategy that meets his or her investment objectives and constraints. I, for instance, follow a dividend growth strategy, meaning I invest almost entirely into companies that have a history of growing their earnings, cash flow, and dividends throughout the business cycle, which greatly lowers my investment risk.

You will have to find out what strategy suits you on your own. A good way to get started is to read financial news regularly and read up on the F.I.R.E. stocks mentioned in this chapter.

8. Don't Follow the Herd

There is a *lot* of group mentality at work in the stock market. When lots of people buy a certain stock and the price rises, other people want to jump on board hoping to profit as well. Being contrarian and having your own thoughts and ideas will serve you greatly in the stock market. Don't mindlessly follow others just because you have heard they are buying a certain stock. Again, do your own research.

9. Stay Humble

You might have a winning streak when making stock investments, and that's great! Maybe you bought the dip in the stock market just at the right time, and the market bounces back, dealing you a boatload of easy profits. That's awesome, but don't get carried away here! Good on you that you made some profits, but the worst thing you could do is become arrogant. You will have losses at some point. Everybody does. Be prepared for it and deal with it in a professional manner.

10. Use Stop Loss Protections

Stop loss orders are orders that can save your butt if the market or a stock unexpectedly tumbles. A stop loss order is a sell order that tells your broker to sell your stock if the stock price falls below a set price. Say you buy a stock at $10 and put it in a stop loss order at $9. This means that in the event that the price of your stock drops below $9, your broker will automatically sell the stock. The purpose of a stop loss order is to limit your losses and protect you against sudden bursts of volatility.

If you make some of these mistakes on your journey to financial freedom, there is no reason for despair. I have made all of the mistakes listed here, many of them more than just once. The important thing is that you learn. Investing is a marathon, not a sprint!

Key Takeaways

- Learning to invest money on your own is incredibly empowering;

- If you desire passive income, you can build your own investment portfolio consisting of high-quality F.I.R.E. stocks that have a history of growing their dividend payouts independent of the stage of the business cycle and the level of interest rates;

- REITs are superb income vehicles for investors desiring high-quality, dependable dividend income;

- *Dividend Aristocrats* are stocks that have raised their dividend payouts for at least 25 consecutive years. Their past dividend growth records strongly suggest that investors will continue to benefit from growing dividend income in the future. *Dividend Aristocrats* and *REITs* are two groups of stocks every income investor should want to own;

- Double down on F.I.R.E. stocks and dollar cost average when these stocks are out-of-favor and the market temporarily loves other stocks;

- Millennial investors have a major time advantage over other investors, meaning they can afford to take more risks;

- Investing is a marathon, not a sprint. When you are investing you are playing the long game. Don't expect immediate results. Start slowly and focus on your long-term goal of financial independence.

CHAPTER 8

PASSIVE INCOME THROUGH REAL ESTATE INVESTING

"If the best time to plant a tree was 20 years ago,

the second best time to plant a tree is today."

~ Chinese Proverb

A nother excellent way for aspiring early retirees to build passive income streams is through real estate. Since you can use other people's money when dabbling in real estate, you can also start relatively fast. While I don't do much real estate investing myself due to the fact that I live in SE-Asia and can't own property outright as a foreigner here, I do have significant real estate exposure through my investments in REITs.

For the purpose of this chapter, however, we are going to discuss *active* real estate investing, which can include a number of different real estate investing strategies: you can buy houses and lease them to tenants (which is the most common way), or you can fix them up and try to flip them for a profit. You can invest in apartments, commercial properties, duplexes, or single-family houses. Since we are all looking for ways to explode our incomes and grow our passive income streams, I am going to focus entirely on the first strategy mentioned here: buying properties and leasing them to tenants.

In its most simple form, you can buy a property in your city and lease it to a tenant who will pay you rent every month. Most often, leases dictate a minimum lease term of one year, which in reality can often be much longer. Most people simply don't want to move every year, meaning landlords are typically looking at substantially longer lease terms. The longer the lease term, the better for you as a real estate investor: long lease terms (1 year or longer) imply little tenant turnover and steady cash flow. And that's just how we would like it.

Tenants that stay put, pay their rents on time, and are not causing any trouble are a landlord's dream because the business is just so simple and straightforward: you buy a property, fix it up (if necessary), and then rent it out. Assuming you have done some basic tenant due diligence, you usually don't have to worry much about your property at all other than repairing a few things here and there every once in a while. If you did a proper house inspection before buying your investment property, it is unlikely that you will have to shoulder any big repair costs that will eat into your future profits, too.

Real estate investing is an excellent way of investing and creating passive income for people that don't like to spend a lot of time on managing and monitoring their investments. You buy the property, fix it up, rent it out, and collect your monthly rent checks… it is as easy as that.

The Five Big Advantages of Real Estate Investing

Like other asset classes such as stocks or bonds, real estate has certain pros and cons that need to be discussed.

One of the biggest cons of real estate investing is that real estate is illiquid. If you want or need to sell your property, it can often take months to find a buyer for your property. You have to advertise your property, show the property to multiple buyers, and then actually close the deal. This typically takes time, which means your money remains tied up in your investment property. Illiquidity is the single biggest disadvantage when it comes to real estate investing.

On the contrary, consider stocks of large companies that trade on a stock exchange; they are typically very liquid. Being liquid means that if you want to either buy or sell a stock, you can expect to immediately find a seller or buyer for it. The stock exchange and your broker will make sure that you almost instantly find a buyer/seller on the opposing side of your trade. Liquidity, hence, can be an issue for real estate investors, especially under circumstances when you are pressured to liquidate your real estate holdings in order to deal with a personal emergency.

On the flip side, however, the are numerous advantages of real estate investing, and the benefits widely outweigh the downside.

Real estate is a cash flow business, first and foremost, meaning you are dealing with hard cash on a monthly basis. You have significant potential to increase the value of your investment property through small and large renovations. You can use other people's money to buy an investment property, meaning you don't have to have all the cash saved up yourself before getting active in real estate. You can utilize depreciation to offset income, and you have a really good shot at benefiting from price appreciation of your investment property over the long haul.

Let's discuss the specific advantages of real estate investing to demonstrate the value this asset class brings to the table for investors that aspire to achieve financial freedom and collect passive income.

1. It's All About Cash Flow

Real estate, at its core, is a cash flow business. You rent your property out for, say, $1,000/month, and that's automatic cash. Every month.

$1,000 in extra (gross) income is a big deal for most people, including me. Of course, you also have mortgage and other costs that you need to factor in. If you go to the bank and get a mortgage loan, you have to make interest and principal payments each month. Say, for instance, that you bought an investment property and that your mortgage payments amount to $700/month. If you rent your property out for $1,000/month, you are still cash flow positive: $1,000 in rental income minus $700 property-related financing costs equals a positive cash flow of $300 that you can use at your discretion. The tenant effectively repays your mortgage for you, which means the tenant is helping you build equity in your investment property.

Of course, this is a simplified calculation and in practice you will have to deal with other expenses as well (maintenance and repair costs, taxes etc.), but the point should be clear here regardless: real estate investing is a great way to produce cash flow/passive income that you don't have to work for.

2. Potential to Create Significant Value

Real estate investors can add substantial value to their properties by making sensible renovations. Most properties can be improved in one way or another, and you often don't even have to spend that much money to increase the value of your properties. You can paint your house, replace old windows, doors and frames, put in new floors, add a modern kitchen with new appliances, and improve the curb appeal by landscaping. The truth is that there isn't a property that *can't* be improved.

Oftentimes, you just have to make basic, cosmetic upgrades to your investment property, such as throwing a coat of paint on your house, windows and doors, and putting in new tiles. This will have a positive effect on the appearance of your property and will allow you to charge prospective tenants a higher rent.

Making value-adding renovations is key for real estate investors that are serious about passive income. For one thing, a newly renovated house or apartment has a much higher appeal to prospective tenants and stands out in the crowd. Secondly, your renovations increase both your cash flow and the value of your investment property.

Say, for example, that you bought an investment property that was previously rented out for $1,000/month. You now make some basic repairs, paint the entire house, put in new tiles, and fit in a new kitchen. Due to the improved condition of your house, you might now be able to rent out your property for $1,200/month instead of $1,000/month. The $200 increase in rent is significant because it adds up nicely over time: $200 more each month in rental income translates into $2,400 additional cash flow per year, or $12,000 more over a five-year period. That's not just small potatoes! Over a five-year period you would make so much more cash from your value-adding renovations that you could potentially finance the down-payment of an entirely new income-producing investment property!

Also, let's not forget that your value-adding improvements will increase the market value of your property. Say that you bought your investment property at 15x gross rental income and paid $180,000 for it ($1,000 monthly rent x 12 months x 15 multiple). Let's assume also that you invested a total of $10,000 into making this property tenant-ready. Since your renovation efforts have resulted in a higher monthly rent of $1,200, the value of your house has now increased to $216,000 ($1,200 monthly rent x 12 months x 15 multiple).

As a result, the $10,000 you spent on renovations have increased your net worth (your total assets minus liabilities) by $26,000: the value of your property is now $216,000 minus $180,000 acquisition costs minus $10,000 renovation costs. That's not bad considering that you just did a little bit of cosmetic work on your investment property, right?

One note on real estate valuation:

Properties are typically valued based on a multiple, or on a so-called *cap rate basis*. A multiple of 15x means that you are paying fifteen times the current annual rent for a property.

A cap rate is simply a yield that indicates your expected rate of return. If you divide the number 1 by the multiple, you will get the cap rate for your investment property. In our example, you will have to divide the number 1 by 15 (our multiple), which yields 6.7%. This cap rate means that you can expect to make a 6.7% gross return on your initial investment.

Here's another way to do the math: You spent $180,000 on the purchase of your property and are about to collect $12,000/year in rental income (before making any modifications). Divide $12,000 in rental income by your investment outlay of $180,000, and you'll get the same result: 6.7% which, once again, is the gross yield on your investment property (before operating expenses, maintenance, taxes, and fees etc.). Professional real estate investors often use cap rates to measure the profitability of their property deals.

3. Use Leverage to Your Advantage

The third advantage of real estate investing is that it allows you to use other people's money. You can buy an investment property for 10 or 20% down, and sometimes you don't have to put down any money at all. When you have a history as a successful real estate investor or have really great credit, banks are more willing to lend you larger amounts of money with relaxed down-payment requirements.

Obviously, using other people's money works greatly in favor of people that seek to build long-term wealth and passive income. If you can buy a $180,000 investment property and just need 10% ($18,000) as a down payment, it makes your project much more affordable. Not a lot of people would be able to make a $50,000 or higher down-payment on a house, for example. Being able to use leverage, in my opinion, is the single biggest advantage of real estate investing; no other asset class allows you to buy assets with so little of your own money.

4. Depreciation

Depreciation is a non-cash expense that you are allowed to take as a real estate investor and that you can use to offset real estate income. The beauty here is that depreciation is just an accounting entry (meaning, it is not a real cash expense), but nonetheless can be used as a deduction against your income. Thus, depreciation translates into lower taxable income and, correspondingly, lower tax payments, which is a nice little side effect for investors that seek to build passive income through real estate.

5. Long-Term Capital Appreciation

Real estate prices have appreciated over the long haul, and that's great news for real estate investors. Real estate prices have increased since the end of the second world war, and even the sub-prime mortgage crisis of 2007 and subsequent Great Recession did not change this trend.

While house prices fell nationwide in the United States after the collapse of the real estate market more than a decade ago, house prices have reached new all-time highs in 2019.

Before the sub-prime mortgage bubble imploded in 2007, borrowers with poor credit could easily get large mortgages to buy properties they really could not afford. Variable-rate mortgages with teaser rates would stipulate a very low interest rate for a short-period of time, say a year, and then reset to a much higher rate. Many borrowers defaulted on their mortgages once the higher mortgage rates kicked in and housing prices started to collapse at the same time. When the speculative real estate bubble burst in 2007 and more and more borrowers defaulted on their mortgages, a chain reaction happened that ultimately threatened to bring down the entire U.S. financial system.

That said, though, real estate prices have recovered from the real estate market downturn a decade ago just like they did after previous market downturns. Over the long-term, a decade or more, real estate investments are likely to increase in value.

A major recession, of course, has the potential to depress real estate prices temporarily, but the long-term performance record of real estate is pretty solid. Importantly, a recession actually increases the number of attractive deals available in the market for more opportunistic real estate investors, whether you want to buy a primary residence or an investment property.

A Proven Model to Build Wealth

I know a lot of people that make a considerable income with rental properties in their home countries. They purchase properties largely from motivated sellers in order to get a good deal and rent the properties out to tenants. Motivated sellers are sellers that are under pressure to sell their properties quickly. There are many reasons for why people are motivated to sell their properties for a price below market value: some people have to move town because they got a new job elsewhere, or they have to sell due to a divorce or sickness.

Motivated sellers are often willing to offer a discount to the prevailing market price in exchange for a fast close. If you have cash at your disposal (or good banking relationships), being able to offer fast cash can greatly reduce your purchase price and increase your initial yield (your cap rate). The cheaper you can buy a property (considering there are no major damages and the property is in good shape), the greater your potential to unlock value and pocket a significant amount of passive income moving forward.

In real estate, a lot of ways lead to Rome. If you are truly looking for passive income, collecting monthly rental checks is the most straightforward way to make money in real estate, especially with single-family homes, as renters tend to stay put and rarely move out. Renting out properties is easy and straightforward, assuming that your property is in good condition and located in a decent part of town.

Rental income is one of the best incomes you can look for if you aspire to retire early and travel the world. People will always need an apartment or house to live and sleep in. Ideally, you start with one property and bootstrap your way to a portfolio of apartments and houses in order to diversify your real estate income. You can and should use rental cash flow from your first investment property to finance the down payment of a second investment property as soon as possible. Doing this will allow you to explode your real estate income in a rather short period of time with a limited amount of risk. Real estate is one of the best, if not *the* best way to build long-term wealth and attain financial freedom.

Key Takeaways

● Real estate is a fantastic way to build long-term wealth and produce recurring cash flow from your tenants;

● Real estate is a great asset class to build wealth with because you can use other people's money. Therefore, depending on where you live and what your credit score is, you don't have to put up a lot of your own money in order to get started as a real estate investor;

● Single-family houses, multi-family houses, apartments, and commercial properties will most likely continue to appreciate in value long-term as the U.S. economy and U.S. population keep growing. Hence, real estate does not only produce recurring rental income, but the asset itself should increase in value over time as well;

● There are other benefits besides recurring cash flow, leverage and long-term price appreciation: you can create value by fixing up properties or remodeling them, and you get to take advantage of depreciation expenses, which lower your taxable income;

● I am not as much of a real estate guy as I am a stock guy, but that's because I am living in SE Asia. If I had the chance, I definitely would invest more of my money in real estate because it is such an attractive asset class for investors seeking passive income. Despite the financial crisis and real estate market collapse in the United States in 2007/8, house prices have recovered to new all-time highs since.

CHAPTER 9

COMPOUNDING

"Compound interest is the eighth wonder of the world. He who understands it, earns it ... he who doesn't ... pays it."

~ Albert Einstein

I n order to achieve your early retirement goals, it is crucially important to understand the fundamental money principle of *compounding.*

Given the importance of this financial concept and given the degree to which it is underrated in public education, I have hesitated for a long time with introducing this fundamental principle as late as Chapter 9. It is so important to understand the concepts of compounding and the future value of money that it would have been well worth it to include them in the first chapter. That being said, though, discussing the power of compounding makes only sense *after* certain concepts of investing have been discussed. Since we have discussed various forms of investing now, let's dig a little deeper into why compounding is so crucial to understand for people that seek financial freedom.

The Power of Compounding

The power of compounding and the implied need for constant reinvestment is one, if not *the* most important financial concept to understand and use to your advantage. Let's go through a very simple example so that you really understand what compounding is, and why it is so powerful.

Assume, you are investing a certain amount of money today, say $10,000 at 3% per year. Your interest income after the first year will be $300 ($10,000 x 0.03). Compounding now means that your investment return (the $300 you received in interest) will also start to produce interest income for you if you reinvest it. If you reinvested the $300 you received as interest in the first year, your total interest income after year 2 will be $309 ($10,300 x 0.03). You made an extra $9 bucks in the second year simply because you reinvested the interest income from the first year.

The total balance after year 2 will be $10,609. If you continue to reinvest your interest, after 5 years of saving you will have $11,593 in your bank account, and $13,439 after ten years. The kicker here is that the **longer** you reinvest your investment returns (interest, bond income, dividends from stocks, cash flow from your rental properties), the **bigger** the impact compounding has on your overall wealth: after 30 years of saving and disciplined reinvesting, your original $10,000 will have grown to $24,273!

Compounding, in a nutshell, means you reinvest your investment returns (interest/dividends) each year and let your investment returns earn additional income as well. It's interest on interest. The longer your investment horizon, the more significant the impact of compounding will be on your total wealth.

Let's go through another example to highlight the effect compounding investment returns has for people that make or don't make regular contributions to a retirement portfolio (the calculation example from below was adapted from J.P.Morgan's Retirement Guide 2019).

Assume we have four investors who save $200 monthly over varying periods of time.

1. **Smart Sally** invests $200 monthly at a 6% average annual return from age 25 to age 65. Total contribution years: 40.

2. **Late Lucy** invests $200/month, just like Smart Sally, but starts a decade later. As a result, she saves and invests from age 35 to 65. Total contribution years: 30.

3. **Knucklehead Kyle** also invests $200 monthly at 6%, but he saves only from age 25 to 35. He gives up on his savings goals after 10 years because he wants to be cool and liked by his peers who spend all of their money. Total contribution years: 10.

4. **Fearful Frank** thinks the stock market is too risky and tries to play it really safe: he invests $200/month purely into money market funds or savings accounts. As a result, he earns only 2% annually. Just like Smart Sally, he saves and invests for 40 years.

Who do you think will come out on top? Of course, it is **Smart Sally**, who understands the importance of saving money regularly and starting early. Smart Sally's portfolio value at age 65 will amount to $393,700.

Next in line: **Late Lucy.** Late Lucy also invests in stocks but waits until 35 to get started, and she pays a very heavy price for starting a decade later than Smart Sally: her portfolio value at 65 is estimated to be $201,100. Postponing to save money and starting a decade later than Smart Sally cost Late Lucy a whopping $192,600 ($393,700 - $201,100)!

Knucklehead Kyle stopped making contributions after just 10 years, but still ends up with a portfolio value of $192,600, which is almost as much as **Late Lucy's** portfolio value of $201,100. Knucklehead Kyle's portfolio value is nearly as much as Late Lucy's even though Late Lucy saved for 30 years and Kyle socked away money for just 10 years. If he kept at it, Knucklehead Kyle would be just as "lucky" as **Smart Sally.**

Lastly, **Fearful Frank** comes in fourth with a portfolio value of only $147,900.

The lessons here, from an investment perspective, are crystal clear, and there are 3 major takeaways from this simple example:

1. You have to start saving and investing money **as early as possible.**

2. You should save money **regularly,** independent of how the stock market is doing.

3. You should invest in higher-yielding assets such as stocks, bonds, REITs and real estate, not in savings accounts in order build long-term wealth and create passive income.

In short, you would want be like **Smart Sally** who saves money consistently and who started early!

If you asked me what the single biggest reason is for why not more people are financially secure and why they remain stuck in the rat race, it is because they don't understand the simple principle of compounding interest. Compounding interest is huge and an absolute game changer!

You may recall that I discussed the *future value* of car payments in Chapter 2 and highlighted the savings potential if you don't own a car. For your convenience, this is the paragraph from Chapter 2 I am referring to:

"The average car payment in the United States is about $523/month which can eat into your budget quite aggressively. Do you know how much $523 invested monthly will be worth in 5 years, if invested, say, at 7%? Well, take a guess ... the answer will shock you because it is $37,460. And, just for fun, if you keep paying the $523/month for new cars throughout your life, you are missing out on $90,000 in 10 years, $267,043 in 20 years, and $615,314 in 30 years. Is your car really worth this much?"

Whether you calculate the future value of your expenses or the future value of your investments, the math is the same. The main difference is that your expenses will be gone forever while your savings will work for you and produce additional income for the rest of you life, if you reinvest your investment returns.

I recommended you to avoid judging your purchasing decisions based on *today's value* ($523 in monthly car payments), but rather in terms of *future value* ($37,460 total value of your car payments). If you put $523 each month into an index fund and don't touch your investments for 30 years, your balance will be $615,314! That's not just chump change, that's serious, potentially life-changing money! The key to making better financial decisions and retiring early is to fundamentally understand the principle of compounding and learn to think in terms of future value of money, not in terms of present-day value of money.

Ask yourself: "How much money are things *really* going to cost me, long-term?"

If you want to know how much money liabilities will really cost you long-term, you can simply utilize a free compound interest calculator on the internet (just type "compound interest calculator" into the Google search field) and see for yourself. Typically, most compound interest calculators require you to make four or five separate inputs: beginning balance (optional), monthly deposit, interest rate, investment period, and tax rate. That's it. Play around with a couple of numbers and calculate the future value of some of your current liabilities, whether its your car payments or your Netflix subscription. The idea behind playing with such numbers is that you truly understand how much things are going to cost you long-term, and how much money you could save by simply investing into income-producing assets or an exchange-traded fund.

Do you know, for instance, that your $13/month Netflix plan (*"Hey bro, it's just $13 per month!"*) actually costs you $15,294 in total (assuming a 30-year investment period and 7% investment return)? Does the $13/month still seem trivial and negligible to you? Small savings made consistently add up to a nice chunk of money in the long-term (I hope you are not surprised here anymore because I am repeating a lesson I already tried to drill into your head in Chapter 2!).

Compounding truly is a game changer. If done correctly, saving money and reinvesting your returns will do the majority of the work for you if financial freedom is your goal.

How to Become an Automatic Millionaire

Some people may initially feel overwhelmed with the breadth of material condensed in this book. It is a lot of stuff to get your head around. There are a lot of definitions to absorb and concepts to grasp, especially in Chapter 6, where I discussed getting started with investing your savings.

You may also remember that I mentioned an alternative approach to building an investment portfolio by yourself: simply invest every month the same dollar amount into an exchange-traded fund and stick with this strategy for a long period of time.

An ETF-based investment strategy is a highly effective strategy that dramatically raises the odds of you retiring as a millionaire. Unfortunately, this strategy is not discussed a lot in the mainstream financial media, and there is a reason for that. The banking, mutual fund, and insurance industries can make a lot of money off of you when convincing you that you need professional advice from highly-paid financial experts with years of experience crunching numbers and analyzing the markets. Banks hire entire research departments in order to project competence and sell you high-priced financial products.

A simple ETF strategy - investing the same amount of money every month into a low-cost ETF such as the Vanguard S&P 500 ETF (ticker: VOO) - will greatly help you build a nest egg over time that you can use to fund your retirement. I, personally, like to invest in dividend-paying stocks because of the passive income they produce for me on a recurring basis, and I need this income to pay my bills. Nonetheless, the ETF strategy referenced here is by far the easiest and most straightforward way to diversify and systematize your wealth building plan ... and, if done long enough, will make you an automatic millionaire!

Let's say you start saving and investing money when you are 20 years old. If you invest $292/month *every month* until you are 65, assuming a 7% investment return, your retirement portfolio will be worth about $1 million.

I think it is important to highlight the simplicity and straightforwardness of this investment strategy once again, which is why I am going to repeat this example one more time to make sure that you fully grasp it: If you contribute approximately $292 each month consistently to an exchange-traded fund for 45 years, starting at 20 years old, you can expect to retire as a millionaire.

If you increase your savings rate and make more aggressive contributions to your investment and retirement accounts, you will be able to retire a lot sooner than 65. The odds of you being able to retire early dramatically increase if you double down on your ETF and 401(k) plan during recessions when stocks are cheap and when you get more bang for your buck.

However, should you decide to start saving and investing money at 30 years old, you will have to invest $603 each month in order to retire as a millionaire.

If you are 40 years old when you start to save and invest, you will have to put away a whopping $1,318 each month in order to retire with a 7-figure nest egg, and you need to save nearly 4.5x as much each month compared to someone who had the foresight to start saving in their early 20s.

The sooner you start to save and invest money, the easier it will be for you to retire early…if you choose to do so.

Unfortunately, as I said before, not too many people know about the math behind these basic investment strategies, but the numbers clearly speak for themselves. If you are suspicious about the numbers presented here, feel free to run the numbers yourself using one of the many free savings goal calculators floating around on the internet. The main problem here is that the financial services industry has no incentive to educate the public about such low-cost, yet highly-efficient investment strategies for the average Joe and Jane out there, because they are in the business of making money. And they make money, first and foremost, when they sell you expensive mutual fund products that have a good chance of underperforming the overall market over the long haul.

An ETF-based investment strategy is the most effective strategy for most people to build retirement savings systematically. Compounding is incredibly powerful and people that desire to retire early and drop out of the rat race would definitely want to take advantage of this money principle.

Key Takeaways

- Compounding, as Albert Einstein said, is the eighth wonder of the world. Understanding it is crucial. The longer you compound, the larger the effect compounding will have on your net worth;

- Reinvesting your investment returns makes a hell of a difference, long-term. You would want to reinvest your dividends, your bond, interest, and real estate income at any opportunity;

- Most people dramatically underestimate the effect compounding has on the future value of their investments. In the example above, **Smart Sally**'s expected portfolio value is nearly double than **Late Lucy's** portfolio value... simply because she started to save money more early;

- One of the best investment strategies, if not *the* best strategy for investors, considering that most active fund managers underperform their benchmark indices, is to simply invest into a low-cost ETF. If you invest just $292/month into an index fund starting at 20, you can expect to retire a millionaire (if you stick to your contributions throughout your life). If you waste a decade and start at 30, you will have to save twice as much, $603/month, in order to achieve the same financial result. If you start at 40, you will have to save $1,318 each month, 4.5x as much as a 20-year old, to retire a millionaire and to make up for lost (compounding) time;

● Winners and aspiring early retirees simply do this: They start early to save money and they save consistently every month!

CHAPTER 10

WHAT'S YOUR F.I.R.E. NUMBER?

"Financial independence is the ability to live from the

income of your own personal resources"

~ Jim Rohn

After reading through the first 9 chapters, I hope that this book has accomplished two major things:

~ ~ ~

1.   I hope that it has fueled your desire to become financially independent and that you will pursue this liberating and worthwhile goal with the endurance and perseverance it deserves;

and,

2.   I hope that the material in this book increased your financial IQ and that you now feel that you can attack the challenge of financial freedom with confidence.

CHRIS MORGAN

The first 9 chapters essentially encouraged you to reset your priorities and shift your mindset in order to become financially independent. Most often, financial freedom does not require an exceptionally high IQ, good business connections, or a six-figure job. To the contrary, it merely requires that you distance yourself from your consumer mindset that has been holding you back for so long and that you adopt an investor mindset instead. The fastest way to achieve financial freedom is to simply make it the dominant goal in your life.

Setting S.M.A.R.T. Financial Goals

This book would not be complete without discussing *your number*. Discussing savings and budgeting hacks is one way to get you started on your journey towards financial freedom, but you ultimately need S.M.A.R.T. money goals. The acronym S.M.A.R.T. stands for goals that are:

- Specific (simple, sensible, significant);

- Measurable (meaningful, motivating);

- Achievable (agreed, attainable);

- Relevant (reasonable, realistic, results-based);

- Time bound (time-based, time limited, time-sensitive).

S.M.A.R.T. goals are goals that are clearly defined, realistic, and relevant to what you want to achieve. If your goal is financial independence, you need to figure out when you want to retire and how much money you need to have socked away so that you can live off of your passive income. In short, you need to figure out what your personal retirement number is.

Everybody has a different number, though. People have different lifestyles, family situations, number of dependents, health conditions, risk tolerances, savings, educational backgrounds, career paths, etc. There is no right number, and no wrong number. With that being said, let's try to figure out what *your* number is.

How Much Money Do You Need to Retire Early?

There are a couple of ways for you to figure out what your retirement number is, i.e. how much money you need to save up in order to drop out of the rat race and live life on your own terms. As I said before, the calculation of your retirement number depends on a number of factors, and even if you compare two persons of the same age, different lifestyle expectations can produce vastly different retirement numbers. There are three different approaches that can help you quantify your F.I.R.E. number.

1. Consult a Retirement Expert or Certified Financial Planner

If you are really serious about F.I.R.E. you can hire a certified financial planner or financial consultant to develop a solid early retirement plan for you and your family. Consulting an expert in the field is a prudent approach to retirement planning and there is nothing wrong with enlisting professional help. This is not required, however.

2. Use a Free Retirement Calculator

There are multiple retirement calculators floating around on the internet that do the calculus for you and figure out how much money you need to sock away in order to live off of your investment portfolio. It can be quite insightful to play around with early retirement assumptions (retirement age, investment return, recurring expenses after retirement, etc.), so play around a little bit and see how such calculators work. I would recommend you to either use Vanguard's Retirement Income Calculator which you can find at www.vanguard.com, or the retirement and savings calculators on www.investor.gov.

3. Rules of Thumb

There are some rules of thumb that can help you derive an indicative value as to how much money you need to have in your investment/savings/retirement accounts in order to drop out of the rat race and enjoy your new life of financial freedom.

One good rule of thumb is to accumulate a nest egg worth 25x your annual expenses. Assume, for example, that your annual expenses total $50,000 (the actual amount is often much less for people that own their primary residences and/or live in countries with low living costs), then your retirement nest egg should be at least $1,250,000 (25 x $50,000).

Of course, this number is just a *rough* guideline, and you need to treat it as such. Whatever nest egg you require depends on your personal situation and, most importantly, your estimated expenses.

My Personal Favorite: The 125% Coverage Rule

My personal rule of thumb for early retirement is this: you should be able to retire early once *your diversified portfolio consisting of income-producing assets (stocks, bonds, real estate) covers 125% of your recurring monthly expenses.*

Again, this is not a set-in-stone rule, but it is another pretty solid rule of thumb, in my experience, that can help you figure out how much money you need to sock away in order to drop out of the rat race entirely, and open up a new, exciting chapter in your life. It is here that your budgeting experience should pay off, too: you should know after completing the budgeting exercise in Chapter 3 how much money you spend, on average, in any given month.

If you regularly spend $5,000/month to cover your lifestyle expenses, your assets (real estate, stocks, bonds) should produce a total of at least $6,250/month ($5,000 x 1.25) in passive income, on average, each month. If your portfolio produces a 6% after-tax investment return, you would need about $1,250,000 in total savings ($1,250,000 x 0.06 / 12).

If you live, for example, in a low-cost country and need only $2,000/month to live very comfortably, your investment portfolio should manage to bring in at least $2,500/month ($2,000 x 1.25) in regular passive income. Once again assuming a 6% after-tax investment return, you would need to sock away about $500,000

($500,000 x 0.06 / 12) to ensure that you can indeed retire early. The excess income of $500 in this example (the difference between $2,500 in income and $2,000 in monthly expenses) is for you to cover unforeseen expenses, pay out-of-pocket medical bills, or cover occasional one-time travel expenses.

My 125% coverage rule is a pretty good rule with which to evaluate your readiness for early retirement because it is both prudent and leaves room for errors and emergencies. If you normally spend about $2,000 each month, the extra $500/month serves either as a cash cushion for emergencies or can be used to funnel money back into dividend-paying stocks or other income-producing assets to ensure a rising standard of living going forward.

Most financial experts recommend at least $1 million in retirement savings. However, *your* number can be less or much more than that, depending on a variety of factors including your personal situation, your health, your family situation, your career choice and income, your lifestyle expenses, etc. The most important thing for you is to get an objective view on your financial situation and just crunch the numbers.

Crunching the numbers is obviously important because it helps you establish a S.M.A.R.T. early retirement goal that is specific and measurable. An example of a smart goal would be to say that you want to build an investment portfolio valued at $500,000 by age 35 or 40.

Once you have nailed down your retirement number, you simply need to follow the conceptual framework developed in this book with the stoicism of a donkey standing in the rain: live below your means, invest at least 10% of your income in income-producing assets or an exchange-traded fund regularly (more if you want to accelerate your goal of financial freedom), double down on stocks or your exchange-traded fund during a recession, and stick to your savings goals no matter what. At the end of the day, achieving financial freedom is more of a persistence and self-discipline exercise than anything else.

How Long Will It Take You to Become Financially Independent?

Personally, I think most people can achieve financial independence within 10-20 years if they make a serious commitment to it and if they don't owe too much debt. If you treat financial independence purely as an option, you will achieve it very late, if ever.

Remember, your actions with respect to saving and spending money reveal without a shadow of a doubt how serious you really are about F.I.R.E. If you keep on wasting money on expensive dining, lavish vacations, unreasonable impulse purchases and cars you can't afford in order to impress other people, your priority is self-indulgence and fixing your low self-esteem, not financial independence.

F.I.R.E. is achievable for people with average jobs and average salaries. *How* you deal with the money you bring in is much more important than *how much* you bring in. If you can't save money when you have little, what makes you think you will ever be able to save money when you have a higher income? The truth is: if you don't save money now, you probably never will!

Once you make financial freedom the dominant goal in your life and get creative about what you have to do in order achieve it, you are already half-way there. Once you have clarity about your financial and retirement goals, it will be so much easier for you to actually achieve them. As a wise man once said, *"The difficulty is not in achieving our goals, it is in establishing them."*

Key Takeaways

- Setting S.M.A.R.T. financial goals is super important. Smart goals formalize your vision and give you direction as well as motivation;

- Calculate your financial goals based on the three methods discussed in this chapter. You can easily calculate how much money you need to save for your early retirement with the referenced retirement calculators from Vanguard and investor.gov;

- A good rule of thumb is to shoot for 25x annual expenses saved up as a retirement nest egg. If you tend to spend $50,000 a year, you need a nest egg of at least $1,250,000 ($50,000 x 25) in order to retire early and maintain your standard of living.

- My personal rule for early retirement is to produce passive income equal to 125% percent of monthly recurring expenses. This figure allows for variance in expenditures, emergencies, as well as vacations.

CHAPTER 11

RELAX WHILE MAKING MONEY

"Is freedom anything else than the right to live as we wish?

Nothing else."

- Epictetus

Early retirement is awesome for so many different reasons. Contrary to popular opinion, none of them really have anything do with money or what money can buy. Early retirement is all about freedom.

Imagine a life where you get to do what you want whenever you want. Nobody gets to tell you what to think and do in your life. Financial freedom is all about living life on your own terms, it is not about being lazy. Living life on your own terms creates greater life satisfaction and happiness. Money buys things, but not happiness. I can't get over the fact how so many people still try mindlessly to find happiness in things and in posing on social media for other people's approval. I may not know you, but I will guarantee that you won't find happiness in this kind of lifestyle, and neither will you attain financial freedom that way.

If you want to achieve financial freedom, my final advice would be to do the complete opposite of what everybody else is doing. Your work colleagues live entirely for the weekend? Find a side hustle. Your friends blow a fortune on nightclubs and restaurants? Save your money and invest it. Your social circle pressures you to be careless with money? Double down on your savings and find new, more supportive friends. Your neighbors want to compete with you about who has the biggest or most expensive car? Catch the bus and make a down-payment on an investment property instead of blowing a small fortune on your ride.

Be smart. And think long-term.

Think about it.

We are told at every opportunity to spend money that we don't have, we are told to live large and above our means, we are told to show off and exaggerate our successes on social media, which pressures us to live an inauthentic, materialistic lifestyle that is, at its core, deeply unfulfilling and meaningless. We take jobs we don't really care about because of the money and status that we and others associate with it. We buy cars and houses that we may not be able to afford. We make stupid financial decisions almost every single day of the week, just to find social approval and acceptance. We are addicted to trying to impress others. For what?

What is your real pay-off for participating in this never-ending circus?

It's time to break out. It's time to free yourself from the thoughts that have shackled you to a lifestyle centered around self-indulgence, instant gratification, materialism, crushing debt, and feelings of despair and hopelessness. It's time to reset your priorities in life and shift your mindset. And it all starts with saving just $1. Today.

Overcoming your impulses will be your greatest challenge on your way to financial independence, much more so than the actual mastery of the money rules discussed in this book.

Good luck!

CHRIS MORGAN

WANT MORE?

Congratulations, you made it! You really finished this book, I am proud of you :)

The purpose of this book was to illustrate how far you can go in life if you follow basic savings, budgeting, and investing principles. You don't have to have a degree from Harvard or another elite university in order to be financially successful and reach financial independence, and neither do you have to have a 6-figure job or start a super-successful business. Those things help, of course, but they aren't necessary to retire early.

As a matter of fact, all you have to do in order to retire early is to do the complete opposite of what everybody else is doing. Save when others spend, invest when others waste, respect money when others disrespect it, and build a side hustle when others blow a fortune on stupid stuff. Remember, it is not about how much money you *earn*, it is about how much money you *keep*! Most people, unfortunately, never learn this lesson.

After having read this book, I hope you have. Sticking to your savings goals, delaying gratification, and pushing back against peer pressure will be your biggest challenges over the short haul. However, as you form new habits of saving, budgeting and investing money, you, too, should be far ahead of the pack in no time. If you have any success stories or any feedback to share - both positive and negative - or if you would just like to get in touch with me, don't hesitate to drop me a message: chris@retiredby35.com, or connect with me through Facebook, Instagram or YouTube (retiredby35).

I also have a favor to ask of you, if you don't mind.

Please leave me an honest review for this book. I am grateful for all reviews because they allow me to better understand my audience and help me refine my message.

Lastly, if you liked this book, check out my website www.retiredby35.com for more resources and advice about early retirement, investing, and personal development.

I wish you all the best for your journey towards financial independence!

Chris, Founder of retiredby35.com

NOTES

- A significant number of U.S. adults lack basic math skills: 2015, American Institute for Research
https://www.air.org/resource/significant-number-u-s-adults-lack-basic-math-skills

- 62% of Adults Don't Understand Inflation: 2018, OECD
https://www.galleonwealth.co.uk/62-of-adults-dont-understand-inflation-heres-our-quick-explainer

- 78% of U.S. workers live paycheck to paycheck: 2019, CNBC
https://www.cnbc.com/2019/01/09/shutdown-highlights-that-4-in-5-us-workers-live-paycheck-to-paycheck.html

- How Many Americans Use A Budget? 2017, Credit Union
https://go.hfcu.org/blog/how-many-americans-use-a-budget

- Here's how much Americans have saved for retirement: 2018, CNBC
https://www.cnbc.com/2018/05/15/how-much-americans-have-saved-for-retirement.html

- 18 Jaw-Dropping Stats About Retirement: 2018, Fool.com
https://www.fool.com/retirement/2018/02/04/18-plus-jaw-dropping-stats-about-retirement.aspx

- This Is the Way You Need to Write Down Your Goals for Faster Success: 2018, inc.com
https://www.inc.com/peter-economy/this-is-way-you-need-

to-write-down-your-goals-for-faster-success.html

- A third of middle-class adults can't afford to pay for a $400 emergency: 2019, CNBC https://www.cnbc.com/2019/05/17/a-third-of-middle-class-adults-cant-cover-a-400-dollar-emergency.html

- How much are cigarettes really costing you? 2010, Pfizer Inc. https://www.quitterscircle.com/sites/default/files/Cigarette%20Time_Cost%20Calculator.pdf

- A $523 monthly payment is the new standard for car buyers: 2018, CNBC https://www.cnbc.com/2018/05/31/a-523-monthly-payment-is-the-new-standard-for-car-buyers.html

- IRS Retirement Topics: 2019, IRS https://www.irs.gov/retirement-plans/plan-participant-employee/retirement-topics-contributions

- My dog was approved for a credit card: 2016, Money Blog https://www.moneypeach.com/opt-out-credit-card-offers/

- Americans rely less on credit cards: 2014, Gallup https://news.gallup.com/poll/168668/americans-rely-less-credit-cards-previous-years.aspx

- Household Debt And Credit Report: 2019, Federal Reserve New York https://www.newyorkfed.org/medialibrary/interactives/householdcredit/data/pdf/HHDC_2019Q2.pdf

- Average credit card interest rates: 2019, Creditcards.com https://www.creditcards.com/credit-card-news/rate-report.php

- What's the Average U.S. Credit Card Debt by Income and Age in 2019? 2019, TheStreet
  https://www.thestreet.com/personal-finance/credit-cards/average-credit-card-debt-14863601

- Get My Free Credit Report: 2019, Federal Trade Commission
  https://www.ftc.gov/faq/consumer-protection/get-my-free-credit-report

- What Is A Good Credit Score? 2018, Experian
  https://www.experian.com/blogs/ask-experian/credit-education/score-basics/what-is-a-good-credit-score/

- The Average Salary By Education Level: 2018, Smartasset
  https://smartasset.com/retirement/the-average-salary-by-education-level

- Salary is the Most Important Job Criterion: 2016, Statista
  https://www.statista.com/chart/6240/salary-is-the-most-important-job-criterion/

- Facebook stock suffers largest one-day drop in history, shedding $119 billion: 2018, CBS News
  https://www.cbsnews.com/news/facebook-stock-price-plummets-largest-stock-market-drop-in-history/

- Billionaires: The Richest People In the World: 2019, Forbes
  https://www.forbes.com/billionaires/#3324d909251c

- Warren Buffett's Shareholder Letters: 1977-2018; Berkshire Hathaway

https://www.berkshirehathaway.com/letters/letters.html
- Buffett Generates $3.7 Billion on 2008 Goldman Sachs Investment: 2011, Bloomberg
  https://www.bloomberg.com/news/articles/2011-03-18/buffett-generates-3-7-billion-from-goldman-investment-made-during-crisis
- S&P 500 Historical Annual Returns: 2019, Investopedia
  https://www.investopedia.com/ask/answers/042415/what-average-annual-return-sp-500.asp
- Vanguard S&P 500 ETF: 2019, Vanguard
  https://investor.vanguard.com/etf/profile/VOO
- 86% of active equity funds underperform: 2016, Financial Times
  https://www.ft.com/content/e555d83a-ed28-11e5-888e-2eadd5fbc4a4
- Active fund managers trail the S&P 500 for the ninth year in a row in triumph for indexing: 2019, CNBC
  https://www.cnbc.com/2019/03/15/active-fund-managers-trail-the-sp-500-for-the-ninth-year-in-a-row-in-triumph-for-indexing.html
- More evidence that it's really hard to 'beat the market' over time, 95% of finance professionals can't do it: 2018, American Enterprise Institute
  https://www.aei.org/carpe-diem/more-evidence-that-its-really-hard-to-beat-the-market-over-time-95-of-finance-professionals-cant-do-it/

- Warren Buffett just won a $1 million bet: 2018, CNBC https://www.cnbc.com/2018/01/03/why-warren-buffett-says-index-funds-are-the-best-investment.html
- How Many Stocks Diversify Unsystematic Risk? 2015, Morningstar http://news.morningstar.com/classroom2/course.asp?docId=145385&page=4&CN
- Realty Income Investor Relations: 2019, Realty Income https://www.realtyincome.com/investors/investor-presentation/default.aspx
- Home Prices Have Reached Record Highs: 2019, Realtor.com https://www.realtor.com/news/real-estate-news/home-prices-hit-a-new-record-high-despite-housing-slowdown/
- Guide to Retirement 2019 Edition: 2019, J.P.Morgan Asset Management https://am.jpmorgan.com/us/institutional/library/retirement-insights-gtr

Printed by Amazon Italia Logistica S.r.l.
Torrazza Piemonte (TO), Italy